S0-EOI-810

TEXT-BOOKS IN MUSIC

BY

THOMAS TAPPER, Litt. D.

FIRST YEAR HARMONY
   100 Lessons for Beginners

FIRST YEAR MELODY WRITING
   For special music students and for use in Public Schools

FIRST YEAR MUSICAL THEORY
   The Notation, Symbology and Terminology of Music

SECOND YEAR HARMONY
   Being the development and completion of the subject as presented in First Year Harmony

FIRST YEAR COUNTERPOINT

FIRST YEAR ANALYSIS (Musical Form)

PRICE, $1.00 EACH

MUSICAL FORM AND ANALYSIS   Price, 75 cents
   (Supplementary Material to "First Year Analysis")

JUST ISSUED

KEY TO FIRST YEAR HARMONY   Price, 60 cents
   (With additional Exercises)

Descriptive circulars sent free on application

For information regarding

CORRESPONDENCE LESSONS

based on these books, address the publisher

THE ARTHUR P. SCHMIDT CO.

BOSTON
120 Boylston St.

NEW YORK
8 West 40th St.

Second Year Harmony

(A Sequel to "First Year Harmony")

BY

THOMAS TAPPER, Litt. D.

LECTURER IN NEW YORK UNIVERSITY, IN THE CORNELL UNIVERSITY SUMMER SCHOOL,
AND IN THE INSTITUTE OF MUSICAL ART OF THE CITY OF NEW YORK

Price, $1.00

THE ARTHUR P. SCHMIDT CO.

BOSTON   LEIPZIG   NEW YORK

120 BOYLSTON STREET   8 WEST 40TH STREET

Copyright, 1912, by ARTHUR P. SCHMIDT
International Copyright Secured

Copyright, 1912,
BY
ARTHUR P. SCHMIDT

A. P. S. 9420

Stanhope Press
F. H. GILSON COMPANY
BOSTON, U.S.A.

PREFACE

This book is divided in two parts.

In Part I, close position is used, and all chords not presented in FIRST YEAR HARMONY are taken up for study.

In Part II, open position is used, and the harmonization of a given soprano is required.

The opening chapters follow a definite plan of presentation. This plan includes:

(a) The chord selected for study, shown and described in both modes.

(b) Tone Study, by the practice of which the student learns the chord, its character, and resolution *through the voice*. The value of this practice cannot be over-stated.

(c) Questions designed to bring the salient facts before the student in question and answer form.

(d) Bass and soprano melodies to be harmonized.

The items that make up the working vocabulary are presented in detail, and many examples are given to illustrate the English text.

In the Appendix will be found some test papers in harmony, which have been set in schools and colleges.

THOMAS TAPPER.

NEW YORK, *December* 4, 1911.

SECOND YEAR HARMONY

PART I

CHAPTER I

THE SUPERTONIC SEVENTH CHORD

1. The first chord to be added to the vocabulary is the supertonic seventh chord. In C major and in C minor this chord appears thus:

2. A seventh chord, being a dissonant tone-group, requires resolution. This resolution may take place in several ways, the most usual of which is found in its progression to the triad of the tone a fourth above its root. Thus, the seventh chord on D, in paragraph 1, resolves regularly to the triad a fourth above D, which is G. This form of resolution, applicable to nearly all seventh chords, is based upon the authentic cadence formula, in which the dominant proceeds to the tonic, thus:

(1)

Note in these examples (1) that the first chord is the dominant seventh of the key, (2) that the second chord is the tonic triad of the key. The bass G moves up a fourth (or, what is equivalent, down a fifth) and the other tones, on the treble staff, connect directly with the tonic triad. The tenor G, in examples (*a*) and (*b*), is common to both chords. The leading tone, B, moves up to C, and the seventh of the dominant seventh chord, resolves down, regularly, to the third of the tonic chord.

3. Applying this form of progression to the supertonic seventh chord, there is produced an exactly parallel resolution:

4. All seventh chords admit of three inversions. (See FIRST YEAR HARMONY, Chapter L, page 131.) In the first inversion, the third of the seventh chord appears as bass tone; in the second inversion, the fifth is the bass tone; and in the third inversion, the seventh appears in the bass.

Thus:

[C major musical example: II$_7$, $^6_5\!_3$, $^6_4\!_3$, $^6_4\!_2$]

NOTE. In C major the supertonic seventh is numbered thus: II$_7$. In minor, a small circle is added, thus: II$^o_7$, to indicate the diminished fifth.

[C minor musical example: II$^o_7$, $^6_5\!_3$, $^6_4\!_3$, $^6_4\!_2$]

5. The full figuring of the inversion is rarely used. $^6_5\!_3$ is generally abbreviated to $^6_5$, $^6_4\!_3$ to $^4_3$, and $^6_4\!_2$ to $^4_2$ or 2.

6. The regular resolution of the fundamental II$_7$ (see paragraph 3) applies also to its inversions, and all follow the authentic cadence formula. (See paragraph 2.)

7. The dominant triad, or seventh chord, often proceeds, not to I, but to VI, making the deceptive cadence. Note that in the authentic cadence resolution, the V$_7$ may appear complete, or without its fifth. In the deceptive form of cadence, however, the seventh chord must be complete to avoid faulty progressions.

8. The deceptive cadence in C major V$_7$ VI, and in C minor V$_7$ VI:

[Musical example showing V$_7$ VI in C major and V$_7$ VI in C minor]

9. This progression, applied to the II$_7$ chord results as follows in C major. It is not applicable in minor as a complete resolution of the supertonic chord, because the third degree in minor is an augmented triad.

C major   *C minor*

II$_7$ III   II°$_7$ III$^+$

10. Seventh chords may appear complete, with root, third, fifth, and seventh, or the fifth may be omitted and the root doubled in one of the upper voices. Hence:

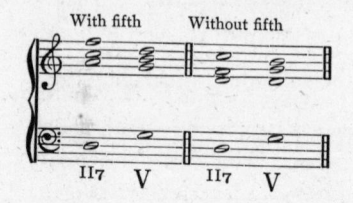

With fifth   *Without fifth*

II$_7$ V   II$_7$ V

TONE STUDY

11. Before the student proceeds to harmonize basses which include this chord and its inversions, he must familiarize himself with it by repeatedly singing the chord and its resolution.

1. Sound with the voice, taking the pitch from the piano, the tonic and its octave:

2. Then the following, using the Italian syllables,* singing slowly:

II$_7$———— V————

3. Then embody the entire group in metrical arrangement:

II$_7$———————— V————

4. Similarly, in C minor, sound the tonic:

5. Then the following, with syllables:

II°$_7$———————— V————

6. Then in metrical grouping:

II°$_7$———————— V————————

7. Sound on the piano the supertonic seventh chord, fundamental position, of the major keys of:
C, A♭, E♭, B, G, F.

* For the application of the Italian syllable names, see First Year Melody, Page 1.

8. Sound on the piano the supertonic seventh chord, fundamental position, of the minor keys of:
E, B, E♭, C♯, F♯.

9. Sound the tonic of each of the following keys, then sing the tones of the supertonic seventh chord ascending, and resolve upon the leading tone, falling to the dominant:
   (a) Major — D♭, E♭, A♭, B♭, F, G, E, C.
   (b) Minor — C, D, G, B, A, F, E, E♭, F♯.

10. Sing the following in the major and minor keys given in Question 8:

C major

I___ V₇___ I   V   I

12. This vocal practice should not be discontinued until the chord has become thoroughly familiar. Once the II₇ chord is grasped mentally in its progression to V, other progressions, which will be shown in succeeding chapters, will be easily mastered.

QUESTIONS

1. What is the interval structure of the II₇ chord in major?
2. What is the interval structure of the II⁰₇ chord in minor?
3. When is a seventh chord in its fundamental position?
4. How many inversions has a seventh chord?
5. Write the full figuring of each of the seventh chord inversions, and its abbreviated figuring.

6. How does the bass move in the regular resolution of a II$_7$ chord?

7. What is the usual progression of the seventh of a seventh chord?

8. Name the major key in which each of these inverted II$_7$ chords is found:

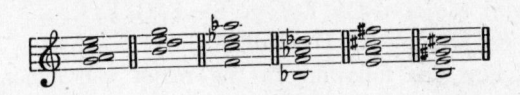

9. What is the authentic cadence resolution?

10. Write the authentic cadence resolution (V$_7$I) in C, A♭, E♭, G♭, and F major; and in B, D, F, E, A, and C minor.

BASSES TO BE HARMONIZED

Harmonize the following, in four parts, close position. First copy the bass correctly, adding the figuring. *Then sing the bass.* When the three upper parts have been added, play at the piano. Finally, proceed thus with every exercise: (This practice should be followed with all written work.)

1. Sing the soprano, playing alto, tenor, and bass.
2. Sing the alto, playing soprano, tenor, and bass.
3. Sing the tenor, playing soprano, alto, and bass.
4. Sing the bass, playing the soprano, alto, and tenor.

Vocabulary:

The triads and their inversions.

The dominant seventh and its inversions.

The II$_7$ and its inversions.

8

Add the bass

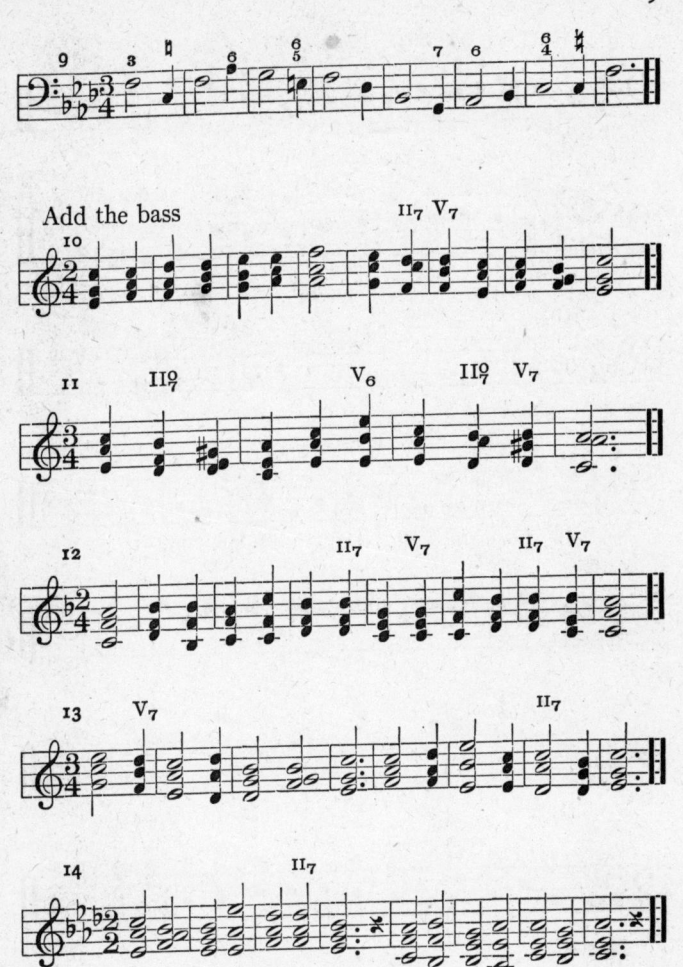

NOTES ON THE PRECEDING EXERCISES

No. 2. Measures three and four, modulation to the dominant. Measure six $^6_5\flat$, passing modulation to the sub-dominant. The tones required above D are f, a♭, b♭,

No. 4. Measure seven the 5♯, requires the triad of D with augmented fifth (a♯) which must resolve up to b in the next measure.

No. 6. Both 6 chords (second and third measures) require the double third.

No. 7. Sixth measure: second chord. The seventh of this chord (b♭) resolves by holding over into the $^6_4$ chord of the next measure.

No. 10. In the first four measures use fundamental triads only; and in sequence.

No. 11. Third measure, second chord, use an inversion.

No. 14. First measure, second chord, the II$_7$ in the $^6_5$ position.

Seventh measure, first chord, the tonic $^6_4$.

CHAPTER II

THE SEVENTH CHORD ON THE SUPERDOMINANT

The seventh chord, upon the sixth degree of the scale, differs widely in effect in the two modes. In the tone study suggested in the previous chapter the student will have noticed the comparative mildness of the supertonic seventh chord, both in major and in minor. Further, he will, by analysis of the exercises, have remarked that the II$_7$ chord is admirably adapted to precede the V or V$_7$ chord. In fact, this progression II$_7$, V$_7$ I is the commonest form of the authentic cadence. Fundamentals rising a fourth, or falling a fifth, are particularly satisfactory because based upon the natural progression of V to I. Hence, as V precedes I, so II precedes V; and in like manner, VI precedes II. Thus:

But, to avoid the awkward progression which results from a series of rising fourths in the bass, the rising fourth is often replaced or expressed by the falling fifth (its equivalent). Hence the above passage is better thus:

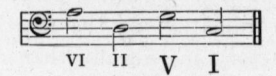

[Musical notation: VI II V I]

That the adaptability of the VI$_7$ chord to precede II is greater in major than in minor, is seen when the tone effect of the chord is closely observed in both modes:

[Musical notation: C major VI$_7$, C minor VI$_7$]

In interval structure the VI$_7$ chord in major is exactly like the II$_7$ in major; both chords consisting of root, minor third, perfect fifth, and minor seventh, a combination of tones that is comparatively mild in its degree of dissonance.

By analysis of VI$_7$ in minor, we find that it consists of a fundamental, a major third, a perfect fifth, and major seventh. The presence of the major seventh produces dissonance so harsh that the chord is less adapted in minor for pure four-part writing than it is in major.

Before taking up the tone study of this chapter, the student should sound on the piano the VI$_7$ in minor, fundamental position and inversions, and listen attentively to the effect of the tone groups in each case:

[Musical notation: C minor VI$_7$ VI$_7\left(\frac{6}{3}\right)$ VI$_7\left(\frac{6}{4}\right)$ VI$_7\left(\frac{6}{2}\right)$]

The presence of the minor second (G–A♭) renders the inversions particularly harsh. Again, the natural progression of the bass (A♭) up a fourth (to D) is not practical with this chord, ordinarily, as the fourth is augmented; hence, less satisfactory melodically than a perfect fourth. Nor may the bass VI rise a second to II° as in the deceptive cadence formula (V VI) owing to the presence of the augmented second from VI to VII° in minor. Consequently, the roughness of the VI$_7$ in minor, in any position, and the impracticability of its progressions taking place as with VI$_7$ in major, make the chord impractical in pure four-part writing as a chord of regular resolution.

TONE STUDY

1. Sound the tone C on the piano, and sing the major scale up and down from that pitch, to establish the key in the mind.

2. Then sing, or play, the following tones, noting the natural progression; that is, the plan of the tone groups, as they are indicated in Roman numerals, below the tones:

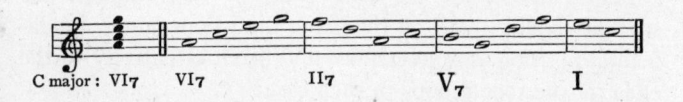

C major: VI$_7$ VI$_7$ II$_7$ V$_7$ I

3. Sing this progression in several major keys, first writing out the chord (in small notes) and the melodic seventh chords (large notes) as is shown above.

4. For comparison, sing the same progressions in minor:

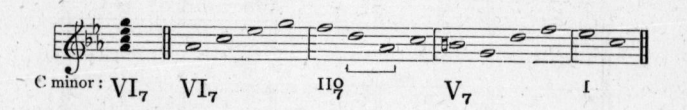

C minor: VI$_7$ VI$_7$ II$_7^{\circ}$ V$_7$ I

5. Sound the tonic of C major again, sing the following inversions, and observe the resolution of VI$_7$ to the triad of II.

C major: VI$_7$ II   VI$_7$ II   VI$_7$ II

6. Write and sing these in several major keys.

QUESTIONS

1. What is the interval structure of VI$_7$ in major?
2. What is the interval structure of VI$_7$ in minor?
3. To what triad does the VI$_7$ naturally resolve (on the authentic cadence formula) in C major, G major, A♭ major, D♭ major, E major, F♯ major?
4. Why is VI$_7$ in minor less practical in pure four-part writing than VI$_7$ in major?
5. In what major key does each of these occur as VI$_7$?

6. Resolve each of these chords (a VI$_7$ or its inversions):

BASSES TO BE HARMONIZED

Vocabulary:

The triad and its inversions : $_6$, $^6_4$.
The V$_7$ and its inversions.
The II$_7$ and its inversions.
The VI$_7$ and its inversions.

6

8 7 6 ♮ 6 6 6♮ 6 7 8 4 3

7

3 6 6 7 ♯ 7 8 4 3 ♯ 8 4 3 5 6 8 6 4

8

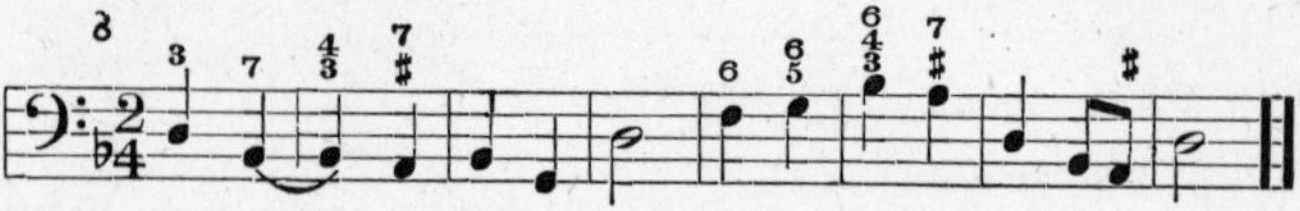
3 7 4 3 7 ♯ 6 6 5 6 4 3 7 ♯ ♯

9

I6 II7 V7 VI6 VII°6

10

VII°6 I6 II°7 V7 II°7 V7

11

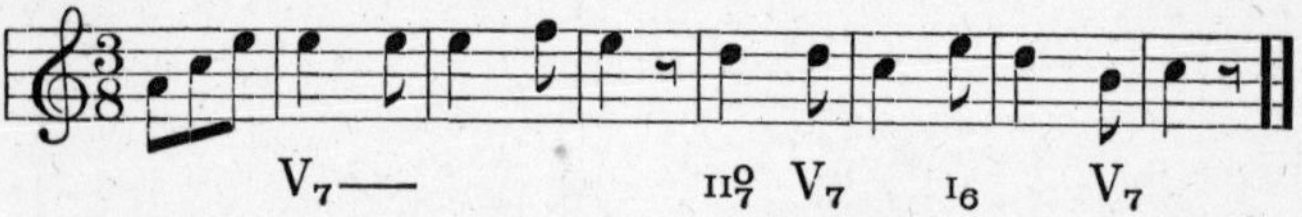
V7——
II°7 V7 I6 V7

12

VI7 II7 V7 VI I6 VI7 II7

NOTES ON THE PRECEDING EXERCISES

No. 1. The 5♯, following the 5 in the last measure but one, requires the dominant triad to appear with augmented fifth a♯.

No. 3. Soprano begins, in first chord, on [musical notation]. In the second chord it moves to b: (third line).

No. 4. Measures four and seven. See note No. 1.

No. 5. Begin thus, in the upper parts:

[musical notation] etc.

No. 6. Second chord. The seventh g, resolves up to a♭.

No. 7. Measure four: The dominant triad (d–f♯–a) is emphasized by the $\frac{6}{3}$ chord. The tones required in the first chord are g–a–c♯.

CHAPTER III

THE SEVENTH CHORD ON THE MEDIANT

C major   *C minor*

III$_7$ III$_7^+$

In the major mode the III$_7$ chord is a comparatively mild dissonance; in minor, it is exceedingly harsh. The figuring of this chord in major shows in the small numeral, III, that to a major triad (root, minor third, and perfect fifth) there is added a minor seventh. In the minor mode, III$_7^+$ indicates, in the large numeral, III with the sign + to the right (III$^+$) that the root, third, and fifth form an augmented triad; to this a major seventh is added.

While the III$_7$ in major is constructed of intervals exactly parallel to those of the II$_7$ chord, there is a greater degree of dissonance in III$_7$. This is probably due to the difference in the fifths, D–A, and E–B in the tempered scale.

In major, III$_7$ may be resolved by either the authentic cadence formula, or by the deceptive. In the former case, the root rises a fourth or falls a fifth; in the latter, it rises to the next scale degree, a minor second above.

C major

III$_7$ VI   III$_7$ IV

The III$_7^+$ in minor may be resolved in several ways; its roughness, however, requires that its dissonant tones enter as passing tones, for smooth progression. Hence it is rarely used, in any position, as an independent chord.

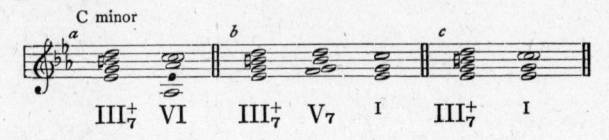

At *a* the regular progression of the bass takes place, the other tones moving to the nearest position in the chord of VI. At *b* the root rises a major second, and the chord of V$_7$ results. At *c* the leading tone ascends, the seventh regularly descends, the root and the third remain stationary. When the dissonant tones of this chord are properly prepared and resolved, the rough effect is reduced to a minimum, and the chord is useful in proper context.

TONE STUDY

1. Sing the tones of III$_7$ in major until their scale relation as a group is clear. Do this in all major keys.

2. Sing the same group in conjunction with the tones of the chord of resolution (VI$_7$) leading through II$_7$, V$_7$, to I.

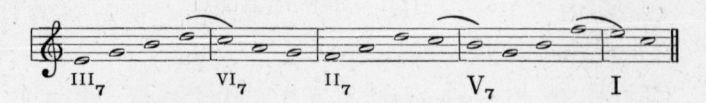

III$_7$ VI$_7$ II$_7$ V$_7$ I

3. Note the regular resolution (authentic cadence formula) of the seventh chords in the following. Sing in all major keys.

III$_7$ VI$_7$ II$_7$ V$_7$ I   II$_7$ V$_7$ I

4. In like manner sing the inversions of III$_7$. Thus:

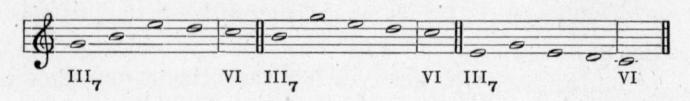

III$_7$ VI   III$_7$ VI   III$_7$ VI

5. Sing each voice part alone, playing the other three; that is, (1) sing the soprano, playing alto, tenor, and bass; (2) sing the alto, playing soprano, tenor, and bass; (3) sing the tenor, playing soprano, alto, and bass; (4) sing the bass, playing soprano, alto, and tenor.

III$_7$ VI

6. In C minor, sing:

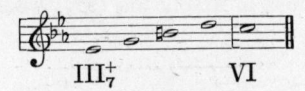

III_7^+ VI

7. And the inversions, thus:

III_7^+ VI III_7^+ VI III_7^+ VI

QUESTIONS

1. What is the interval structure of III_7 in major?
2. What is the interval structure of III_7^+ in minor?
3. Why is III_7 more dissonant than II_7 in major?
4. To what two triads may III_7 regularly resolve, in major?
5. Why must III_7^+ (in minor) enter with especial preparation of its dissonant intervals?
6. In what major key is each of these chords found?

7. In what minor key is each of these chords found?

8. What is meant by preparation of the dissonance? (See Introduction.)
9. What is meant by resolution?
10. Construct on the following fundamentals: C, E♭, F, A, G, B♭, a II_7 chord in major; a II_7^o in minor; a VI_7 in major and in minor; a III_7 in major and a III_7^+ in minor.

BASSES TO BE HARMONIZED

Vocabulary:

The triads and their inversions.

The V_7, and its inversion.

The II_7, VI_7, $III_7^{\emptyset}$ and their inversions.

NOTES ON THE ABOVE BASSES

No. 1. First measure, second chord: the dominant of A minor.

No. 2. Fourth measure, second chord: this is the augmented triad (G B D♯). The D♯ leads upward to E in the following chord. Fifth measure, second chord: The chord is C G B♭, dominant seventh of F major. The seventh, B♭, resolves on A in the next chord.

No. 6. Fourth measure, second chord: G♯ in the alto, moving to A in the next measure. Fifth measure: The $\textit{4}$ requires C♯ in the dominant seventh chord on A; A C♯ E in the upper voices.

No. 7. Fourth measure: The E♭ of the first chord moves up through E to F in the next measure.

No. 8. Fourth measure, second chord: dominant seventh chord of F minor. The tones in the upper voices are C G B♭.

MELODIES TO BE HARMONIZED

2

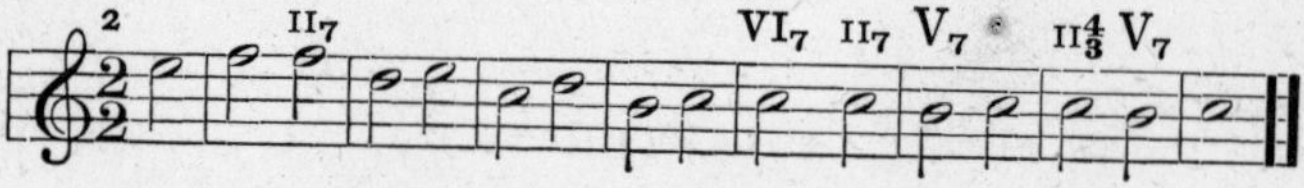
II_7
VI_7 II_7 V_7
II^4_3 V_7

3

V^6_4 I_6
I^6_4 V_7
VI_7 II_7 I^6_4 V_7

4

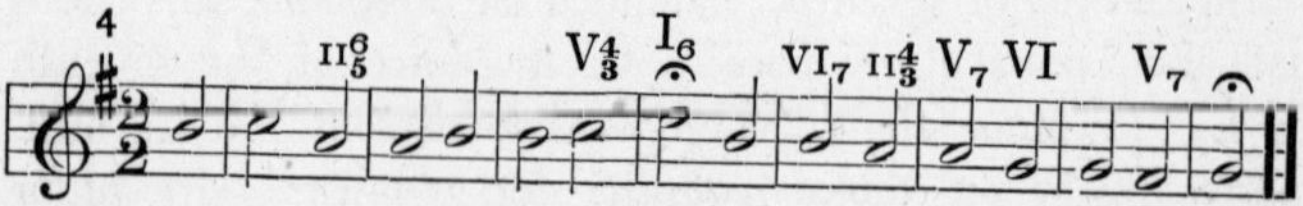
II^6_5
V^4_3 I_6
VI_7 II^4_3 V_7 VI
V_7

CHAPTER IV

THE SUBDOMINANT SEVENTH CHORD

In major, the IV$_7$ consists of root, major third, perfect fifth, and major seventh. Sounded on the piano, this chord is harsh, particularly because of the force of the seventh F–E. In minor, the IV$_7$ chord consists of root, minor third, perfect fifth, and minor seventh; and because of its minor seventh (joined to a minor triad) it is smoother than the corresponding major scale seventh chord.

The IV$_7$ chord cannot make the authentic cadence resolution in either mode, as the interval a fourth above is, in both modes, augmented. Consequently, it follows the deceptive cadence resolution, and moves up one degree to the triad of V. Thus:

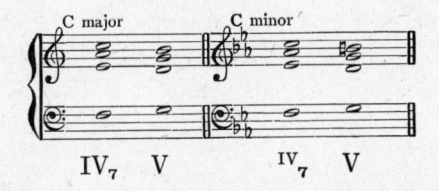

This chord appears to best advantage when the third or fifth of the IV$_7$ is in the soprano. When the seventh is in the soprano the resolution of IV$_7$ to V produces fifths. The seventh chord must always be complete when it resolves a degree upward; that is, in the deceptive cadence progression.

TONE STUDY

1. Sing the IV$_7$ chord in all major keys, with resolution to V.

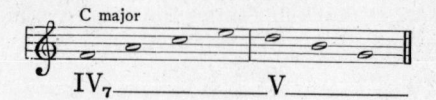

2. And in all minor keys:

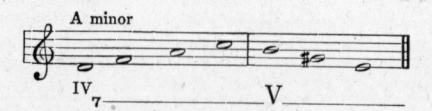

3. Sing the resolving IV$_7$ through V to I in major and minor:

C major

IV$_7$ —————— V$_7$ —————— I

A minor

IV$_7$ —————— V$_7$ —————— I ——

4. The following illustrates the use of this chord in major. Play the exercise, then sing each voice part in turn, playing the other three, as explained on page 20.

C major

I IV II$_7$ V$_7$ I IV$_7$ V V$_7$ I IV VII$^\circ$ VI II$_7$ V$_7$ I

5. The next example illustrates the use of IV$_7$ in minor. Play and sing as directed in No. 4.

C minor

I IV II$^\circ_7$ V$_7$ I IV$_7$ V V$_7$ I IV I I II$_7$ V$_7$ I

QUESTIONS

1. What is the interval structure of IV$_7$ in major?
2. What is the interval structure of iv$_7$ in minor?
3. Which is the more dissonant, and why?
4. Why is the authentic cadence progression not available with the IV$_7$ chord?
5. What tone cannot appear in the soprano of IV$_7$ in its progression to V? Why?
6. Write the fundamental positions and inversions of IV$_7$ in these major keys: C, F, A♭ D♭, G, B.
7. And in these minor keys: C♯, F♯ G♯, A, E, F, B, D.
8. In what major key is each of these the IV$_7$?

9. In what minor key is each of these the iv$_7$?

EXERCISES

Vocabulary:
    The triads and their inversions.
    The V$_7$ and its inversions.
    The II$_7$, VI$_7$, III$_7$, IV$_7$ and their inversions.

BASSES TO BE HARMONIZED

29

JADASSOHN

MELODIES TO BE HARMONIZED

NOTES ON THE PRECEDING EXERCISES

No. 1. Fifth measure, the seventh (c) of the first chord rises to d.

No. 8. Measures three and four are in sequence with one and two.

No. 9. Third measure, first chord, must appear with doubled third.

No. 11. Second measure, second chord, VI.

No. 11. Third measure, second chord, the bass in E, modulating to F major.

CHAPTER V

THE SEVENTH CHORD ON THE LEADING TONE

The chord, in both modes, is a mild dissonance, the minor vii$°_7$ being somewhat less harsh than the major vii$°_7$, owing to the presence of the diminished seventh from the chord fundamental (leading-tone).

Many theorists present the leading tone seventh chord as the dominant ninth chord, with root omitted. The chord in its complete form of five tones, is shown in the following example:

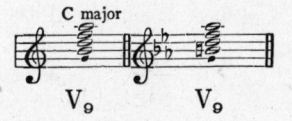

Employed in four-part writing, the V_9 chord must appear with one of its tones omitted; the omitted tone is usually the fifth. The Tone Study work, and the basses for harmonization given in this Chapter will treat this chord as a seventh chord. In Part II, this chord as the V_9 will be studied.

Interval analysis of vii$°_7$ in major, shows that it consists of a root, minor third, diminished fifth, and minor seventh. In minor, the intervals above the root are a minor third, diminished fifth, and diminished seventh.

From the fact that the VII$°_7$ has for its root the leading tone, it invariably makes the deceptive cadence resolution; that is, the root following its usual strong impulse (as leading tone) rises to the tonic. The chord, however, may resolve a fourth up, in major, after the authentic cadence formula, in sequential passages; that is, when the bass moves in regular intervals. Thus:

I   VII$°_7$ III   VI$_7$ II   V   V$_7$ I

Except in sequential passages, this chord usually resolves upon the triad of the tonic. Thus in C major:

VII$°_7$ I   VII$°_7$ I   VII$°_7$ I

1. Sound the tonic of C major, and sing the VII$°_7$ and its resolution:

VII$_7$ —————— I

2. Sing this group in all major keys.
3. Proceed likewise through the minor keys with the following:

VIIo_7 _____ I ____

4. In both modes, in this rhythmical form:

I _____ VIIo_7 _____ I

5. Sing the inversions, testing the pitch from time to time at the piano:

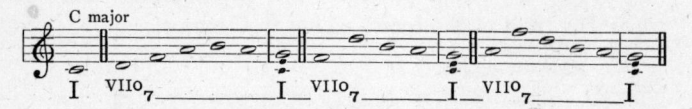

I VIIo_7 _____ I__VIIo_7 _____ I__VIIo_7 _____ I

6. And similarly in C minor.
7. Sing the diminished seventh in the following keys, continuing the practice until the interval is familiar:

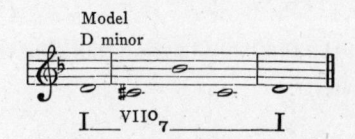

Model
D minor

I__VIIo_7 _____ I

C, F, E, D, A, B, F♯, B♭ minor.

QUESTIONS

1. What intervals occur in the minor scale (harmonic) that are not found in the major scale?

2. What is the interval structure of the diminished seventh chord (VII$^{o}_{7}$) in this inversion?

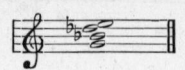

3. To what minor key does each of these chords belong?

4. Which is the milder dissonance, VII$^{o}_{7}$ in C major or in C minor, and why?

5. Write on the dominant of the following keys, the V$_9$ chord; first as a five-tone chord, then as a four-tone chord:

        Major — B, C♭, D♭, G, F, D.
        Minor — B♭, E♭, A, A♭, C, E.

6. When may the VII° in major progress to the triad of a fourth above?

7. Why, ordinarily, does it not make this progression?

8. What other seventh chord in major progresses to the triad of the next degree above?

BASSES TO BE HARMONIZED

Vocabulary:

        The triads and their inversions.
        The V$_7$ and its inversion.
        The II$_7$, VI$_7$, III$_7$, IV,$_7$ VII$^{o}_{7}$, and their inversions.

1

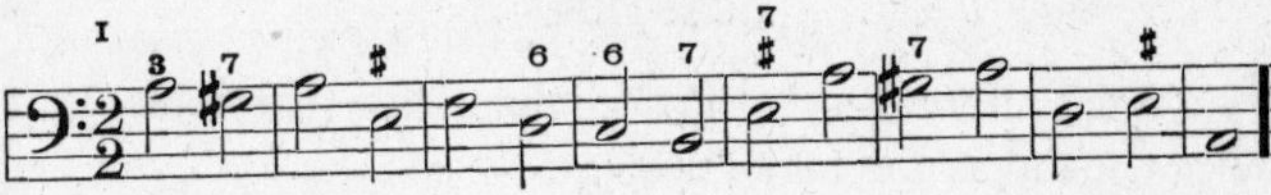

2

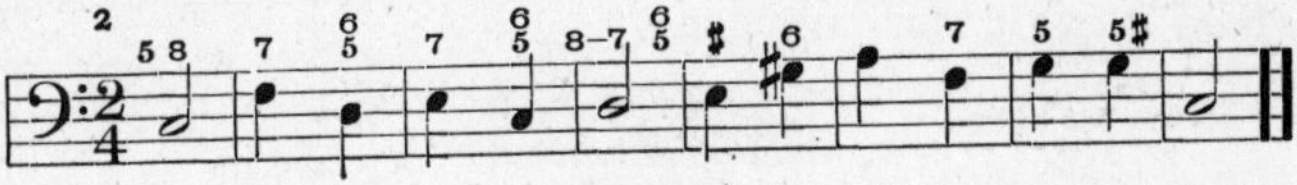

3

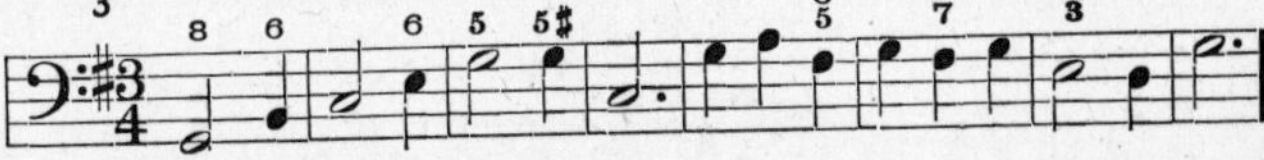

4

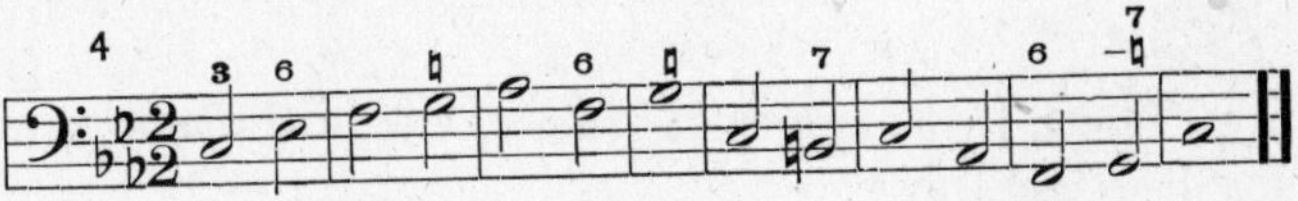

5

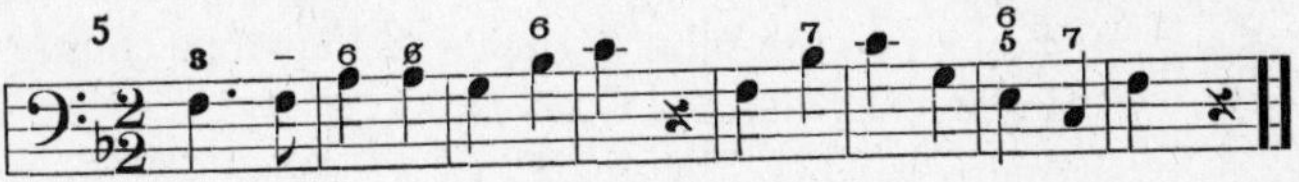

6

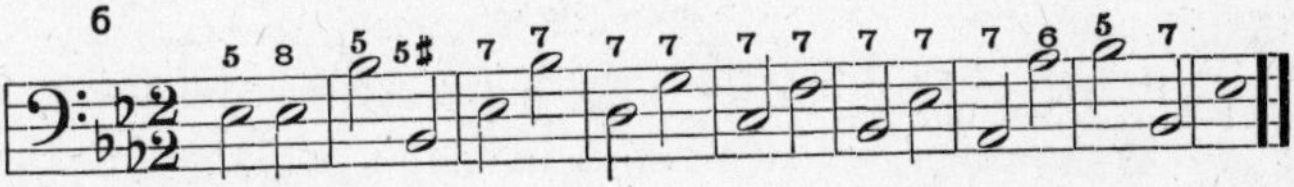

Dr. Paul

7

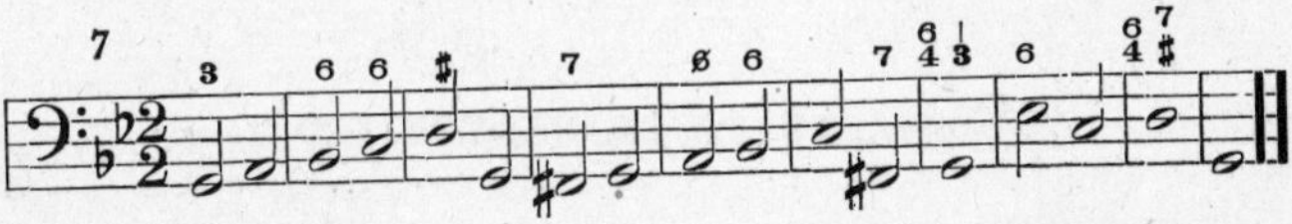

8

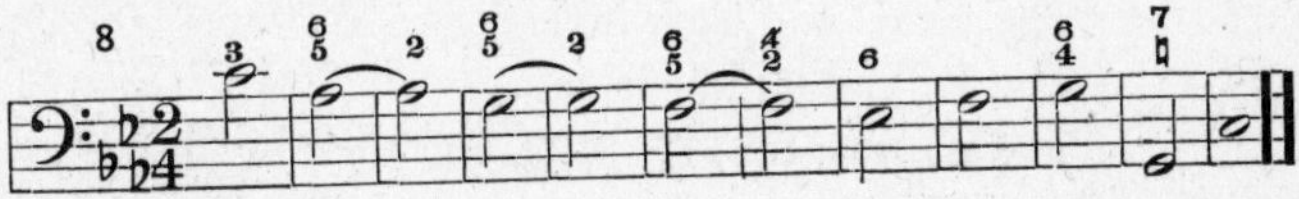

MELODIES TO BE HARMONIZED

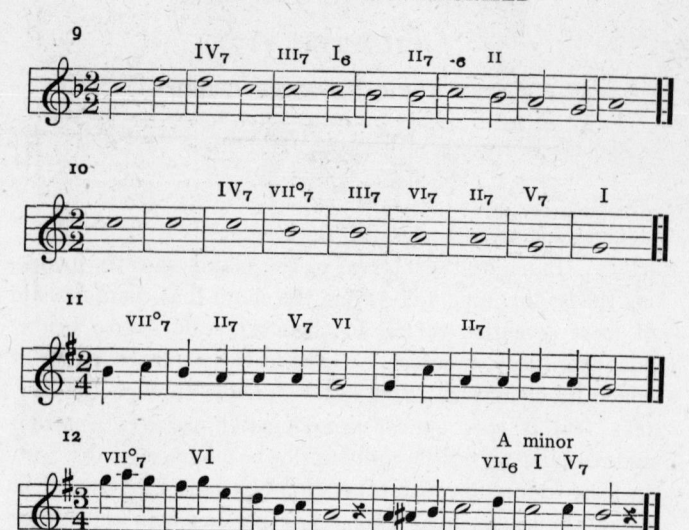

CHAPTER VI

THE TONIC SEVENTH CHORD

The tonic seventh chord in both modes is a harsh dissonance. In major, the interval of the major seventh, including the leading tone, takes from the chord that characteristic of most sevenths, to fall to the next scale degree below. This chord may, however, be used in two ways, by either of which its dissonance is made less forcible through the context. (*a*) It may appear in sequential passages, entering and resolving as satisfactorily as do the milder sevenths. (*b*) In close connection with other chords, triads or sevenths, in which the leading tone enters as a passing note and brings the I_7 into evidence with smoothness. Thus:

While the I_7 in major is thus practical even in pure part writing, the corresponding chord in minor is not. By close chord connection the I_7 may be made to enter and to give a passing suggestion of its independent character. Thus:

I   V   I$^+_7$ VI

See Chapter VII of this book for further explanation of this and other extremely dissonant sevenths.

In interval structure I_7 in major consists of a major triad and a major seventh. In minor, it consists of a minor triad and a major seventh. In both modes, the seventh has a strong tendency to resolve upward, being the leading tone; it may be led downward in major, but not in the harmonic minor scale, for, in the latter, the progression of an augmented second from the leading tone to the sixth degree of the scale is unsatisfactory.

Note the use of this chord in the following example:

I I_7 IV   II II_7 V   III III_7 VI   II   I V_7 I

While the second chord in measures one, three and five appears as independent seventh, the passage is merely a succession of triads, in a two-measure sequence group, the groups being closely connected by a passing tone that, in the above example, gives the impression of independent seventh.

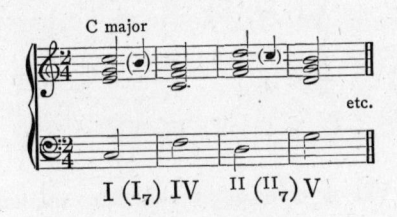

I (I₇) IV   II (II₇) V

TONE STUDY

1. Sing the tones of I₇ in order, and observe the tendency of the seventh.

I₇ ———— IV ———

2. But observe in singing the following that, through the momentum of the sequence, I gives the impression of resolving to IV naturally.

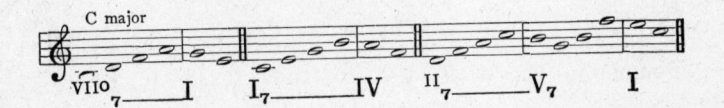

VII°₇ —— I   I₇ —— IV   II₇ —— V₇   I

3. Sing the following, and observe that when the tones of the triad on I continue through the leading tone, descending, that the seventh in I_7 appears as passing tone:

4. Sing the following, observing the pronounced tendency of the leading tone to ascend:

5. Sing the next example, observing the tone group of I_7 and also that the underlying I_7–IV resolution brings the leading tone down to A naturally:

III_7 _____ VI II_7 _____ V I_7 _____ IV

6. All examples given in the above questions should be practiced in several keys.

QUESTIONS

1. Write the I_7 in
    C, G, B, D♭, A♭, E♭, major.
    F, D, A, C, F♯, E♭, minor.

2. What two forms of triad are contained within the I_7 in major?

3. What two forms of triad are contained within the I_7 in minor?

4. Write and resolve the I_7 in the keys of C, G, B, D♭, A♭, E♭, major, in four parts, resolving the chord (*a*) upon the triad of the fourth degree; (*b*) upon the triad of the second degree.

5. Locate each of these chords in a major or minor key, as I_7:

6. Chromatically alter one tone in these chords, to produce a dominant seventh in each case:

BASSES TO BE HARMONIZED

1. All triads and their inversions.
2. All seventh chords and their inversions.

NOTE. — From this point the harmonization of melodies, in close position, will not be required.

In Part II, melodies alone (soprano, alto, or tenor part) will be given for harmonization in open position.

Beginning with Chapter VII, harmonic analysis of part music is introduced and continued to the close of Part I.

CHAPTER VII

REVIEW

The basses to be harmonized which are given in this chapter, present a general review of the fundamental and inverted seventh chords, thus far studied. The chromatically altered triad (with augmented fifth) is introduced, and an occasional modulation to a nearly related key.

It is suggested, in harmonizing these exercises, that the student adopt the following process:

1. Write the soprano throughout.
2. Then add the alto.
3. Lastly, add the tenor.

Each part should be sung as it is completed, and the whole tested, when finished, by the chord progressions.

QUESTIONS

(Applicable to the Exercises of this Chapter.)

1. In which of the following exercises is the augmented triad used, as a chromatically altered chord?
2. Where are consecutive seventh chords used sequentially?
3. What cadence form is employed in No. 6, fourth measure?
4. Where is the passing modulation employed?
5. When may the vii$°_7$ proceed on the authentic cadence formula (that is, its root rising a fourth)?

44

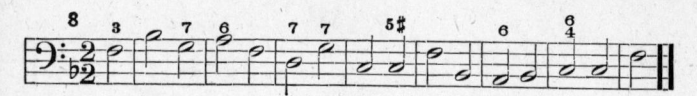

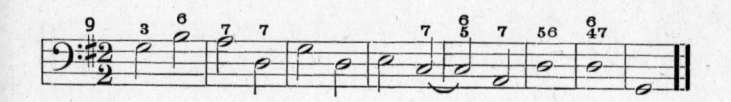

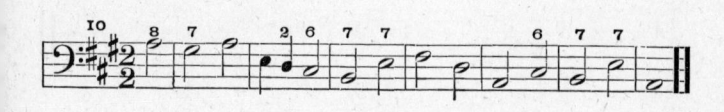

ANALYSIS

In each chapter, from this point to the end of the book, chord analysis is taken up. This work will require frequent references to the preceding chapters of this book, and to the text of FIRST YEAR HARMONY.

LUDWIG VAN BEETHOVEN

1. What is the key?
2. What is the key at the end of the first phrase?
3. In what key is the second phrase?
4. Where is the $\frac{6}{4}$ chord used?
5. In what key is the augmented second E♭–F♯ found?
6. What seventh chords are used in this example? Give the root of each.

CHAPTER VIII

NON-CADENTIAL RESOLUTIONS

Thus far we have observed the seventh chords chiefly in their cadential progressions. The root rises a fourth, following the authentic cadence formula, or to the next scale degree above, following the deceptive cadence progression. In nearly all cases the seventh has been regarded as a tone that proceeds downwards in its resolution. Thus:

In major:
  I$_7$ proceeds to IV or II
  II$_7$ proceeds to V or III
  III$_7$ proceeds to VI or IV
  IV$_7$ proceeds to V (to VII° only rarely and through the impulse of sequence)
  V$_7$ proceeds to I or VI
  VI$_7$ proceeds to II (see note on IV$_7$)
  VII$_7^{\circ}$ proceeds to I (see note on IV$_7$)

In minor:
  IV$_7$ (see Chapter V)
  II$_7^{\circ}$ proceeds to V
  III$_7^+$ (see Chapter III)
  IV$_7$ proceeds to V
  V$_7$ proceeds to I or VI
  VI$_7$ (see Chapter II)
  VII$_7^{\circ}$ proceeds to I

In practical music all these chords may be used in many other ways. The most dissonant seventh chords may be gradually introduced and made to pass over to the other less dissonant chords before resolving.

Through the motion of the other voices, the seventh itself (of a seventh chord) may resolve:

1. Downward (regularly) or
2. Upward, or
3. It may remain stationary.

Careful observation of the progressions found in the exercises at the end of this chapter will show that these progressions are practical. Note the following:

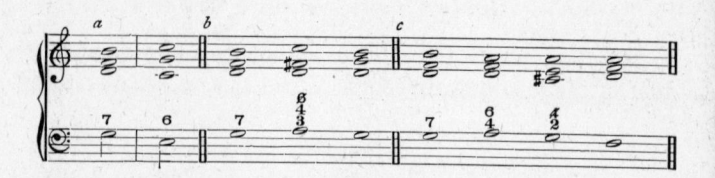

At *a*, the seventh (F in the alto) moves up because the bass proceeds to E, the tone of resolution. Should F also proceed to E, the seventh would resolve in two voices and produce hidden octaves.

At *b*, the seventh, F, moves up to F♯, producing another V_7 chord, which, in turn, progresses regularly, its seventh C, resolving on B, in the soprano.

At *c*, the seventh, F, remains stationary and passes over in the third chord to the V_7 of D minor.

Other examples of the same, and similar resolutions:

At *a*, the seventh (E♭) proceeds upward to E.

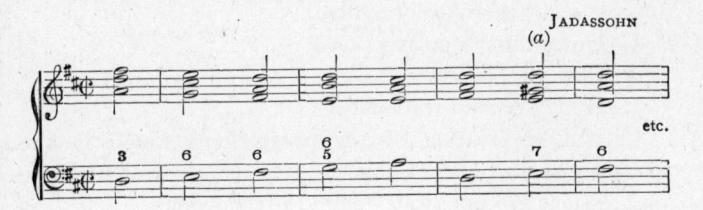

At *a*, the seventh (D) remains stationary and becomes the root of the following six chord.

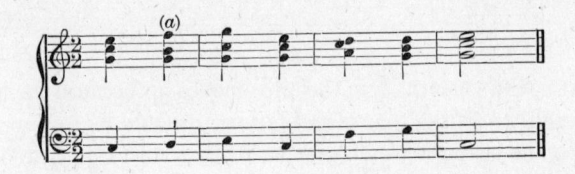

At *a*, the seventh (F) may move either up to G, or down to E.

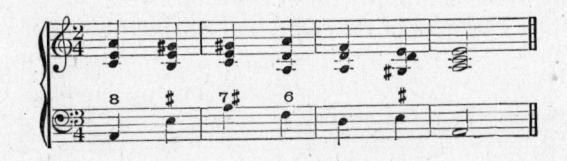

At *a*, the seventh (G♯) moves up to A.

BASSES TO BE HARMONIZED

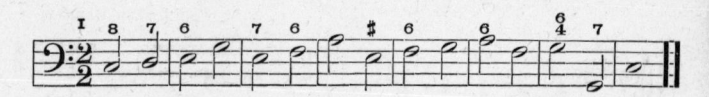

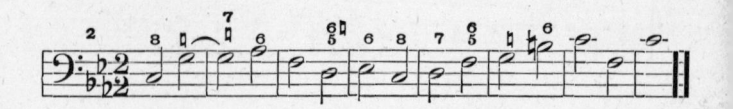

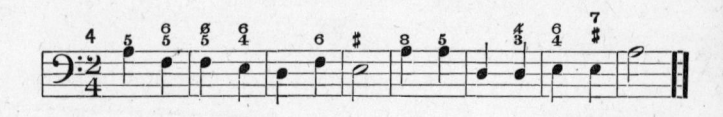

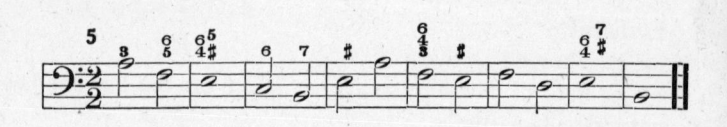

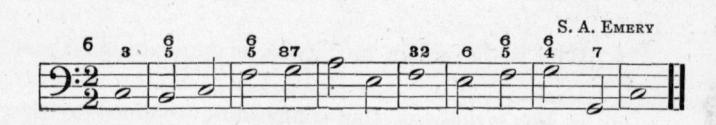

ANALYSIS

Sir Joseph Barnby

1. What is the key?
2. Why may the second chord (first measure) be in the $\frac{6}{4}$ position?
3. What modulation occurs in A major, through the tone E sharp?
4. Through D sharp?
5. Bass of measure six: what effect on the key has D natural? C natural?
6. What chord prevails through the penultimate measure?
7. Why is the unison used twice in measure one (bass clef)?
8. Is the melody of this composition confined to the soprano?

9. Are any of the chords in close position?

10. Why may the third of the tonic triad be doubled in the second measure?

11. What is the purpose of having the parts cross in measure four?

12. How many dominant seventh chords are used? What is the key of each?

CHAPTER IX

CHROMATICALLY ALTERED CHORDS

In four-part writing, of simple character, any one of the melody lines may be enriched by introducing chromatic tones as modification of the chord. The following example is of simple chords throughout and illustrates the basis of chromatic alteration:

In this, the melody lines may be given character and greater impulse by introducing chromatic tones, a process with which the pupil is already somewhat familiar. (See p. 15.) The first chord to be so modified is the triad, and the strongest melodic tendency may be given to it by allowing its fifth to proceed chromatically upward. In the next example, this modification occurs at the points marked with the 5♯.

Such modification of the triad rarely produces a modulation. The preceding example begins and ends in C major. At the points where the 5♯ occurs an enrichment of the melody line occurs. The effect of these chromatically altered chords is to emphasize the following chord as an integral part of C major.

A triad may be chromatically altered, not only in its fifth degree but in its third. The following are the various chromatic inflections that may be used.

Major triads: 5♯ or ♭3.

Minor triads: 5♯ 3♯.

Diminished triads: (6 chord position) 5♯, 3♭. All these are illustrated in the examples that follow:

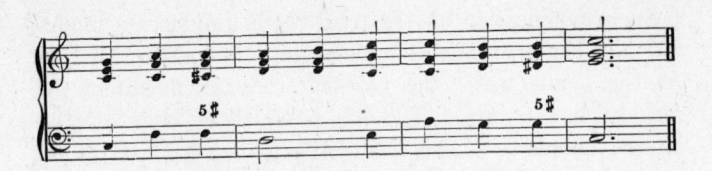

The use of chromatically altered chords produces a thorough bass notation that is complicated beyond what we have hitherto seen. While some of the signs used in this chapter have already appeared, the following list may be of service for reference:

1. 2 4 5 etc. A stroke through a numeral is equivalent to the ♯ sign (as applied to the tone in the key of the exercise).

2. ♮ ♯ ♭ used above a note refer to the modification of the third.

3. 5× means a double sharp to the fifth of the bass note.

4. $\substack{5\ 7 \\ \sharp\ -}$ The short line under the seven means to carry the sharp in both chords.

5. $\substack{3 \\ 5} - 5$ The line means continue the previous chord $\left(\substack{3\\5\\5}\right)$ as second chord; the 5 requires the same chord again $\left(\substack{3\\5\\5}\right)$ but with chromatically altered fifth.

TONE STUDY

1. The impression of the chromatically altered chord in its progression is best perceived, in this exercise, by singing the given notes, sounding at the same time on the piano, the fundamentals indicated below the melody line.

[Musical notation in F: I — IV — V₇ — I]

[Musical notation in G: I IV V I]

2. Sing the following in several major keys:

[Musical notation in A♭: I — IV V I]

3. Sing each voice part separately, in the following example, at the same time playing the other three parts.

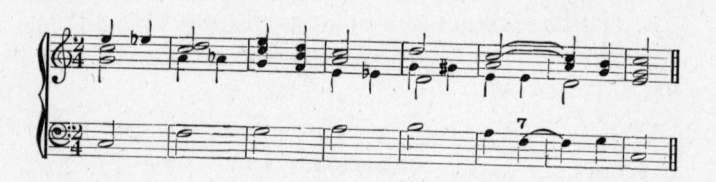

[Four-part musical notation example]

GENERAL RULES REGARDING CHROMATICALLY ALTERED CHORDS

1. The sharp sign requires the modified tone to move upward to the next scale degree.
2. Similarly, the flat sign requires the modified tone to move downward to the next scale degree.
3. The chromatically altered tone must not appear in more than one voice.

4. Rules for chord progressions, thus far learned, are not set aside through the use of chromatics.

5. A chromatically altered fifth, if held into the next chord *as new leading tone*, creates a modulation:

C I^a V₇ I

6. If the chromatically altered tone appears in the bass, it must not be used in the upper voices.

7. Sharp five, as non-modulatory progressions, cannot be used in the triads of VI and III in major, owing to the minor seconds between three and four, and seven and eight.

8. Flat three cannot be used in the triads of VI and II in major, owing to the minor seconds between three and four, and seven and eight.

QUESTIONS

1. How must the sharp inflex be resolved?
2. How must the flat inflex be resolved?
3. Which triads, in major, cannot take the sharp five? The flat three? Why?
4. Why must the altered tone be restricted to one voice?
5. Do chromatically altered chords always produce a modulation?
6. What is the value of the chromatically altered chord in four-part writing?

7. In what manner may chromatic alterations be made to produce modulation?

8. When does the augmented triad appear as a natural to the key?

9. When may the diminished triad admit of its fifth being led upward, by the sharp?

ANALYSIS

1. First measure. What two tones are chromatically altered?

2. What chord is emphasized by this alteration?

3. What is the effect of the F♯ in measures three and four?

4. Measure seven: How far does the influence of the first chord extend? What is this chord?

5. What is the first chord in measure nine?

6. What is the first chord in measure eleven? Where does the D♭ resolve?

7. What is the effect of the F♯ in measure thirteen?

8. What is the position of the triad in measure fourteen?

CHAPTER X

CHORDS OF THE AUGMENTED SIXTH

By chromatic alteration the augmented sixth may be made a component of three chords: (1) the first inversion of a triad; (2) the first inversion of a seventh chord; (3) the second inversion of a seventh chord; that is, of a 6, $\frac{6}{5}$, and $\frac{6}{4}$.

The presence of the augmented sixth in these chords is indicated by a stroke through the 6, thus ϐ; or by the sharp sign following the six (according to the key), thus 6♯.

These chords may appear either in major or minor. They may be made to enter so as not to change the key, or they may be used for modulatory purposes.

The following illustrates the chord of the augmented sixth in C major:

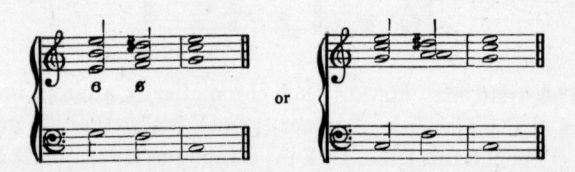

In C minor:

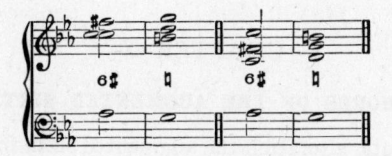

In all instances the augmented sixth chord is a chromatically altered *minor triad*. The following illustrates its use in G major:

S. JADASSOHN

G I - V₇ I a IV III⁺ V₇ I e V₇ VI G II₇ V₇ V I

The derivation of the augmented sixth chord, from the minor triad, shows (1) the minor triad itself, (2) the minor triad with raised fundamental, (3) the first inversion in which the third of the triad becomes the bass tone, and the raised root appears in one of the upper voices. Thus with the minor triad on D:

This triad may appear, thus chromatically altered, in the keys of C major (II); A minor (IV); F major (VI); D minor (I). Though this triad, D–F–A, is found in B♭ major, it may not be thus chromatically altered in that key. The D♯ conflicts with the sub-dominant, E♭, and cannot be led upward to E.

The chord of $\frac{6}{3}$ may be employed in major and in minor.

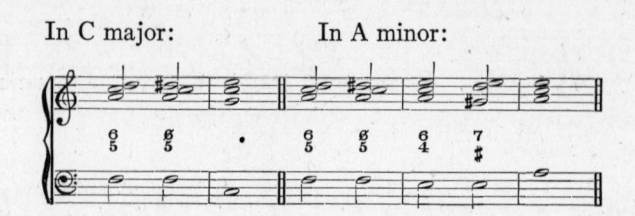

In C major: In A minor:

Likewise the $\frac{6}{4}{3}$ chord is equally available in both modes:

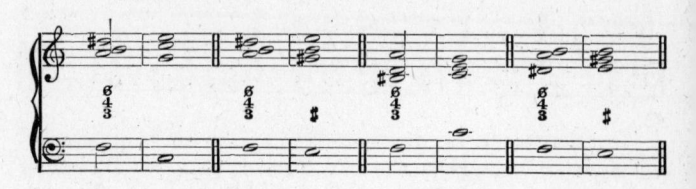

BASSES TO BE HARMONIZED

63

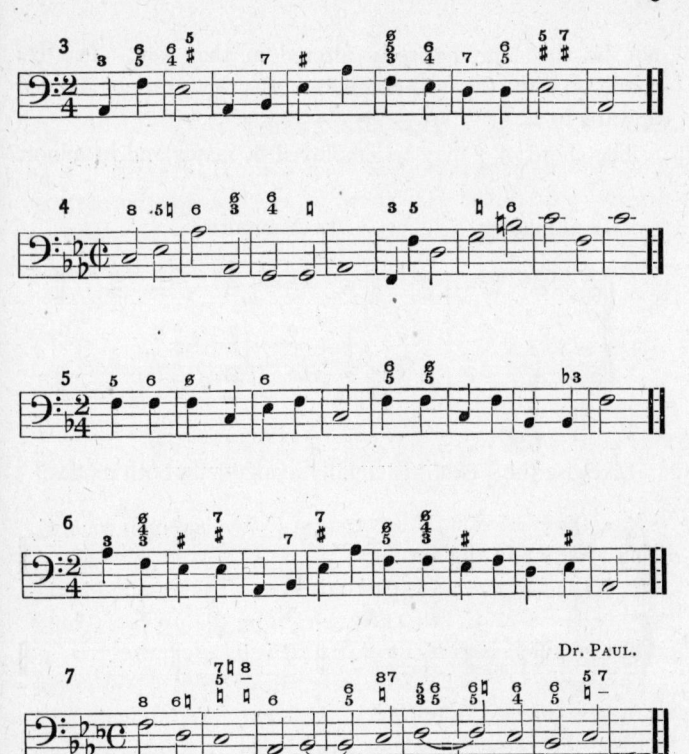

Dr. Paul.

CHAPTER XI

THE SUSPENSION

A tone may be prolonged from a chord of which it is an integral part to the next chord in which it does not belong, by the nature of the chord structure. This prolongation causes a dissonance, which requires preparation and resolution.

At *a*, the triad of G follows that of C, the common tone, G, being retained in the alto.

At *b*, the soprano tone, C, holds over, so as to sound in the triad of G. The C being tied over from the previous chord is thus prepared, and its motion to B is its resolution.

The soprano C (in Ex. b) merely delays the B (third of the G major triad). In order to indicate, in thorough bass figuring the presence of the suspension, it is necessary to figure the C–B independently *from the given bass note* G.

Thus: Ex. c.

      8   4 3

C   I   V

A great variety of suspensions (and hence of thorough bass figuring, indicating suspensions) may occur. The entrance of practically any tone of a triad, of a triad inversion, a fundamental seventh chord, or of its inversions, may be delayed and thus create a suspension.

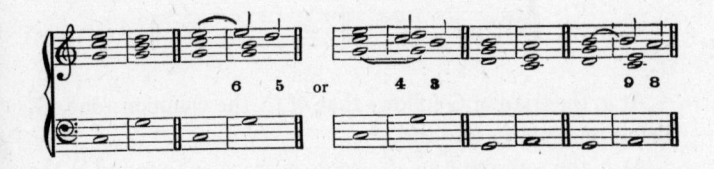

The following general rules for suspensions must be carefully observed:
- (a) The suspended tone must be prepared and resolved in the same voice-part.
- (b) The regular and desirable progression of chords must not be disturbed by the suspension.

ANALYSIS

Name each chord, as to root.
State whether the chords are fundamental or inverted.
What figures are required to indicate the suspensions?

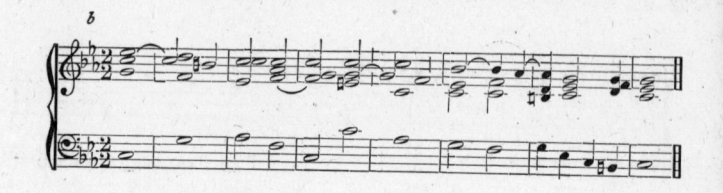

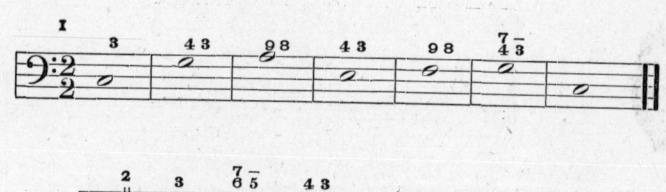

67

CHAPTER XII

THE SUSPENSION

The following bass should be harmonized in all three positions of the first chord, that is, with three, then five, then eight, in the soprano. Note the effect in the soprano, alto, and tenor.

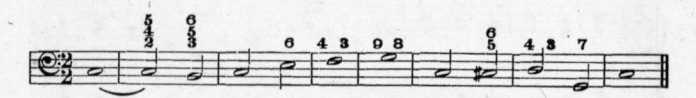

Care must be taken, as previously stated, to prepare and resolve the suspended tone *in the same voice-part*.

Suspensions are also available in the bass. Thus:

The figuring $\frac{5}{2}$ is, in full, $\frac{5}{3}$ or $\frac{5}{2}$ according to the position of the sixth chord with doubled fifth or doubled root.

ANALYSIS

Play the following. Add below each bass note the figuring to represent the chord.

Note, and mark the suspensions.

CHORAL

J. S. BACH

CHORAL

J. S. BACH

JOHN STAINER

JOHN STAINER

71

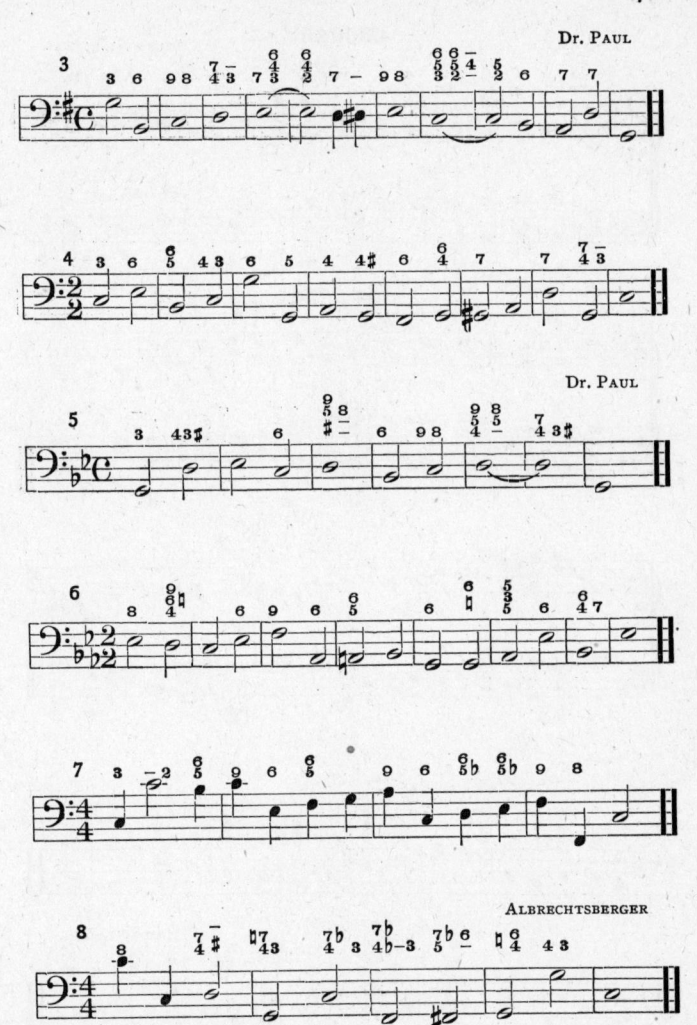

ALBRECHTSBERGER

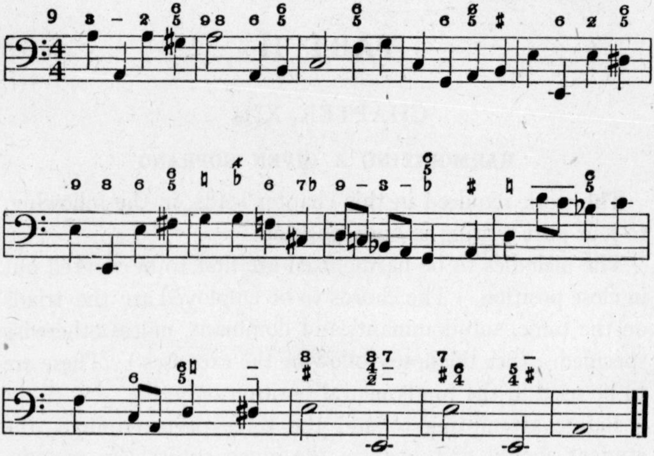

PART II

CHAPTER XIII

HARMONIZING A GIVEN SOPRANO

The work required in this chapter leads, in the following, to four-part writing in open position.

The melodies to be harmonized are first to be worked out in close position. The chords to be employed are the triads on the tonic, sub-dominant, and dominant, unless otherwise specified. (See the notes following the exercises.) These are to be used in the fundamental position only.

Before attempting to add the three parts required, the student should first analyze the given subject, or melody. First sing the melody, in order to establish its tones firmly in the mind. Then note the following:

1. The initial chord is always the tonic.
2. So, too, is the final chord.
3. The chord next to the last (the penultimate chord) is V.
4. A skip in the melody is always along the chord in which the two tones occur.
5. As only three chords are used (save where otherwise specified) the application of the preceding rule will be easy.
6. A tone repeated frequently requires a change of chord.
7. When a tone occurs three times in succession, the first and third chords will be the same; the second chord will differ.

APPLICATION OF THESE RULES

Sing this melody:

1. The key is C major.
2. The first and last chords will be C–I.
3. The penultimate chord will be V.
4. In the fifth, sixth, and seventh measures, skips occur. The skip in measure five, E–C, consists of two tones in the tonic chord; hence, both will be harmonized by I. The same applies to the skip, C–G, in measure six. The skip in the seventh measure, A–C, consists of two tones in the sub-dominant chord; hence, both will be harmonized by IV.
5. The first tone C occurs three times in succession. As the first chord must be the tonic, the third will repeat it; but the second chord must differ; hence, IV.
6. In measure five C is repeated. The chord is fixed by the skip from E to the first C (second beat). The third beat may change to IV.
7. With this form of analysis completed, next proceed to write in the bass, keeping its tones within an octave.

8. Never allow the bass to make two skips of a fourth or of a fifth *in the same direction*.

The above subject, harmonized in four parts, close position, will appear thus:

MELODIES TO BE HARMONIZED

Proceed in like manner with each of the given subjects below. As other chords than I IV V are sometimes required, read the note on each subject before deciding the triads to be employed.

76

NOTES ON THE EXERCISES

No. 1. At *a*, use the triad of II. At *b*, the V_7 chord.

No. 2. At *a*, use the chord of A♭ (VI). Remember the necessary form of doubling in VI, in minor, following V. At *b*, use the triad on IV.

CHAPTER XIV

OPEN POSITION WITH PRIMARY TRIADS

Close position results when the three upper voices are grouped in, or within, the compass of the octave. This form of writing is familiar to the student from his experience with the exercises up to this point.

Open position results when the tone range from soprano to bass is more or less evenly distributed. In open position it is often necessary for a chord or two to appear in close position. This occurs when the soprano runs low, or when the bass runs high.

In the following example, the distribution of tones illustrates open position:

In harmonizing the subjects given at the end of this chapter, in open position, the following general rules should be carefully observed:

1. The tone range from soprano to bass must be evenly divided among the four voices.

2. Hence, alto and tenor should not, as a rule, be widely separated.

3. Nor should the alto and soprano be widely separated.

4. The bass may depart from the tenor with more or less freedom, the only restriction being that it shall still keep within its own compass.

5. No voice part may proceed melodically through two fourths or two fifths in the same direction. The resulting seventh or ninth is always unmusical.

(a) Two fifths *(b)* Two fourths

The following example illustrates the use of the primary triads in open position:

When the number of chords used in an exercise is limited to three, as in this case, it is inevitable that one voice shall be more or less monotonous. When the chords are more freely introduced, greater melodic variety is possible in each of the four parts.

As a rule, the use of the primary triads fundamentally, rarely brings about concealed fifths or octaves of objectionable kind. In fact, the student may regard it as a fairly safe rule that hidden consecutives involving the primary triads alone, seldom sound badly if one voice proceeds diatonically; but similar consecutives which result from the use of secondary triads, or a combination of the primary and secondary triads, must be scrutinized with more care.

GENERAL RULES

The following general rules apply to all the subjects given at the end of this chapter as a basis for Written Work:

1. The first and last chord of each exercise will be the tonic triad.

2. The penultimate chord will be the dominant.

3. All chords required in this lesson are in the fundamental position unless otherwise specified.

4. In case the first inversion is used, that is, a chord of the sixth, its use will be limited to those chords in which the third itself does not appear in the soprano.

5. In chord progression, I may proceed to IV or to V. IV may proceed to V or to I. V may proceed to I (very rarely indeed to IV).

6. In the exercises at the end of the chapter the slurs used in the first few examples indicate chord repetition. Note that the slurs are later on omitted, it being assumed that the student will remember that all skips are along the chord line.

ANALYSIS

In the following examples, primary triads only are used. They occur fundamentally and as chords of the sixth. The chords are numbered consecutively throughout for ready reference.

The key is F major.

No. 1. Tonic triad, fundamental position.

No. 2. The skip in the soprano from C to F, requires the repetition of I.

No. 3. Dominant triad, fundamental position.

Nos. 4-5. Tonic triad. In No. 5 as a six chord.

No. 6. Sub-dominant triad.

No. 7. Sub-dominant triad, as a six chord.

No. 8. Tonic triad.

No. 9. Dominant triad, making a half cadence. Note the melodic direction of soprano and bass, throughout the first phrase.

Nos. 10, 11, 12, 13. The Tonic triad. No. 10 being the first chord of the phrase is best used fundamentally. No. 11 having the third in the soprano cannot be used as a six chord. No. 12 is in the six chord position. No. 13 is fundamental.

No. 14. Sub-dominant, as a six chord.

No. 15. Tonic triad.

No. 16. Dominant triad, making with No. 17 an authentic cadence.

83

V IV

NOTES ON THE EXERCISES

No. 1. Transpose to G minor.
No. 2. Transpose to F minor.
No. 3. Transpose to A minor or to A♭ minor.
No. 4. Transpose to D minor.
No. 5. Transpose to B minor.

CHAPTER XV

THE TRIADS ON VI AND II

In the exercises of this chapter, the Triads on VI and II are introduced.

The triad on VI may be approached from I, or it may follow V.

The triad on II may be approached from IV, or it may proceed to V.

In the structure of the bass, the cadential progressions (authentic and deceptive forms) suggest the more direct form of procedure.

Roots rising a fourth or falling a fifth are good.

Roots rising one diatonic degree are generally good. (But the triad on VII° may not be included in this.)

Roots rising a fourth, by way of a third, are good. Thus:
I–III–IV.

The triad on II is much used in the authentic cadence group:

II V I, or II I$_4^6$ V I.

The use of VI proceeding from V, and of II in the cadence group, is shown in this illustration from Beethoven:

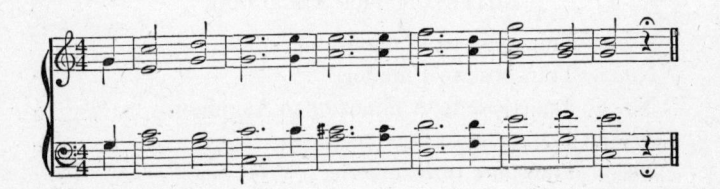

SUBJECTS TO BE HARMONIZED

No. 1. Fourth chord. VI is approached from V. In measure five, VI moves to II, and II, in turn, to V. The cadence group (last three chords) II V I.

No. 2. In what position must the third chord be written to move to II (fourth chord)?

No. 3. The second chord is V. Why?

What form of cadence occurs at the end of the first phrase?

Measure 6, II follows IV and proceeds to V.

No. 4. Transpose to B major.

No. 5. Transpose to G minor.

ANALYSIS

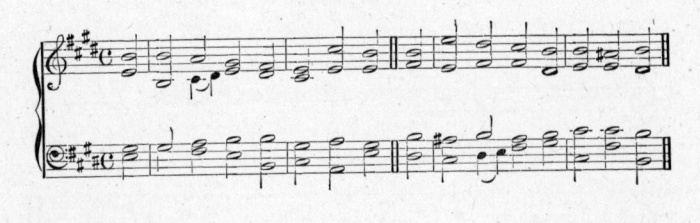

1. Name each chord and its position.
2. What modulation occurs?
3. Explain the use of each six-chord.
4. Note the use of the triads on II and VI.
5. Why is the unison (tenor and bass) used in the second chord?
6. What seventh chords are introduced?

NOTE. — While the examples selected for Analysis present freer use of chords than is specified for the written work of the chapter, they still offer not only abundant illustrations of the use of certain chords, but also serve as models for part writing.

In every illustration, note:

1. The distribution of tones throughout the total compass from bass to soprano.

2. The occasional use of a chord in close position.

3. The simple and direct manner in which modulation is effected.

4. The melodic independence of each voice part.

The student should not confine his studies in harmonic analysis to the single example given in each lesson. If he will play the four-part arrangements, such as those given in the *Choralbuch* of August Haupt, he will appreciate how rich the combinations of four voices may be made when only simple harmonies are employed.

Further, it is admirable to play, for the purposes of analysis, simple piano compositions of the best composers. Nothing serves better, for this purpose, than the Sonatas, by W. A. Mozart, and the easier works of J. S. Bach. The first impression the student will receive on analyzing these works, is that *comparatively few chords are used*. These few chords are, through the impulse of melody and rhythm, spun out and prolonged. Direct and natural modulations provide color and contrast. Most of the secondary chords (except II) are used invariably as passing chords, or they result from the use of passing tones proceeding from one primary chord to another. In fact, the usual chord simplicity of works of the classical school reveals, on close analysis, a wonderful effect produced by simple means. Modulation, suspension, and the use of passing tones of various kinds are always sufficient to leave the simple chord-background undisturbed.

Note in the analysis of the Mozart Sonatas, the absence of many of the secondary seventh chords in direct use. They appear, if at all, only as passing chords.

The subject of passing tones is generally included in a harmony textbook of this grade, but the subject is so easily mastered in the second to the fifth orders of Counterpoint that it is deferred for treatment in the author's First Year Counterpoint.*

In all analysis of chord procedure, the student should make constant reference to the Table of Progressions given at the end of this book.

---

* See also First Year Harmony, Chapter LVII.

CHAPTER XVI

THE FOUR-SIX CHORD

When triads are used exclusively in the fundamental position, the chord succession is stiff and angular. The voice part is invariably confined to so narrow a tone range that it loses any aspect of independent melodic progression. The soprano stands out as the most individual part, and the bass is confined to roots alone.

By employing the six chord as a substitute for the fundamental position, much greater melodic variety is secured. The six chord is never employed as first or final chord, and rarely as penultimate chord. It is available elsewhere *when the third of the triad is not used in the soprano*.

Hence, with primary triads especially, the presence of root or fifth in the soprano discovers a possible employment of the first inversion; but the progression to and from a possible six chord must always be considered.

As a rule, the six chord may be regarded as the equivalent of the fundamental triad to be availed of in certain instances to improve the melodic trend of the alto, tenor, and bass.

The second inversion of the triad (four-six chord) is introduced in this chapter. This chord has three distinct uses: (1) it may appear on the first of the measure in cadence groups; (2) on the non-accented part of the measure as a passing chord; (3) on any part of the measure following its own fundamental position.

This chord gives particular prominence to the bass, and its use, in conjunction with the six chord, affords considerable melodic variety to the voice parts.

The following exercises illustrate the use of the second inversion of the triad:

No. 1, in F major, should also be harmonized in F minor.

No. 3, in E major, should be transposed to E minor.

No. 5, in A minor, should be transposed to A major.

These five exercises will afford ample preliminary practice for the study of the four-six chord if it be accompanied by considerable analysis.

ANALYSIS

QUESTIONS

(The measures are numbered)

1. What is the key?
2. What passing tones are used in measure 1?
3. What inversions occur in measure 1?
4. Measure 2, what cadence form?
5. Measure 3. What triad is used as a $^6_4$?
6. Measure 4. Cadence?
7. Compare with measure 1.
8. Measures 6 and 8. Note the $^6_4$ as it proceeds through the dominant, to the tonic.
9. Measure 7. What key is used in passing?
10. Measures 9–10. Key?
11. Measure 12. Key?
12. Measure 15. Where has this measure occurred before?
13. Measure 16. Why is this varied from measures 2 and 6?

The student should count the number of fundamental chords employed in this selection and compare with the total number of inversions. Note, also, the comparatively infrequent use of passing tones and of seventh chords.

Play soprano and bass (omitting alto and tenor) and note the use of opposite and similar motion between these two parts.

Why is opposite motion, as a rule, to be preferred?

Study the measures in which other keys than the tonic are suggested or introduced.

What keys are closely related to that of the key-note of this selection?

What is meant by Tonic minor? Relative minor?

From the use of passing tones in this selection construct a definition of this device.

What is the difference between a modulation and a suggested key?

What keys are most easily reached from C minor? From D major?

CHAPTER XVII

THE SEVENTH CHORDS

In the following exercises, the chords of V_7 II_7 and IV_7 are employed. Transpose Exercise 1 to G minor; Exercise 3, to A minor, and Exercise 5, to F minor.

All rules hitherto given for the preparation and resolution of sevenths should be carefully reviewed.

The seventh of a seventh chord is prepared when it appears in the previous chord as a consonance. In the case of the milder sevenths (minor and diminished), the seventh itself is often satisfactorily prepared by being approached by conjunct motion.

A seventh may resolve on one of several ways. Regularly, it should move one diatonic degree downward. But it may remain stationary, or even move up a major second or an augmented prime. In the latter case, the effect of dissonance may be transposed to another voice, or the movement of resolution taken up elsewhere than in the voice where the seventh occurs. Examples of these resolutions are found in Part I of this text.

The dominant seventh is a comparatively mild dissonance. The II_7 is a natural precursor of V_7 and the formula II_7 V_7 I is frequently met with in cadence groups.

The sub-dominant seventh is harsh, and the entrance of the seventh must be carefully prepared. The IV_7 moves naturally to V or V_7 or to the four-six on V. (See Exercise 3.)

The seventh chords introduced in the following exercises may be employed fundamentally or as inversions. It must be remembered that used fundamentally there is less freedom in the motion of the parts, while with inversions, the voices, particularly the bass, gain much melodic independence.

ANALYSIS

J. S. Bach.

1. What is the key?
2. The chords are three voiced throughout; two tones in the right hand, group themselves with each bass tone.
3. Place under each bass tone, the Roman numeral, as shown in measures one and two.
4. Measure 4, what form of scale?
5. Measures 5 and 6, what key?
6. Measures 7 and 8, what key?
7. Is sequence employed?
8. Measures 13 and 14, what key?
9. In what key is the final cadence?
10. First beat, first measure, what is the d?
11. Third beat, first measure, what tone of V is omitted?

GENERAL REVIEW

1. Explain preparation of a dissonance. Resolution.
2. Why are preparation and resolution necessary?
3. (*a*) What are the principal uses of the four-six chord?

(*b*) Which triad is not used in this position?

4. How do inverted chords influence the melodic structure, in four-part writing?

5. What triads and seventh chords are used in the authentic cadence?

6. What bass progressions are most satisfactory?

7. What are hidden consecutives?

8. When are hidden consecutives objectionable?

9. Which are the most dissonant seventh chords?

10. Are they frequently used in music of the classical school?

11. Does instrumental music present as frequent change of chord as choral music?

12. What are the most direct modulations (through key relationship) from G major?

13. What is meant by a passing modulation?

14. When may close position be employed in open harmony?

15. When may the unison be employed between two parts?

16. What are passing tones?

17. What do you understand by "classical school"?

18. What composers are prominent in this school?

19. What name is applied to the school of Johann Sebastian Bach?

20. Define chorale, sonata, consonance, dissonance, rhythm.

CHAPTER XVIII

THE NINTH CHORD

The following exercises should be harmonized by the students in two ways: (*a*) In simple chord progressions; (*b*) embodying the various chords specified by the numerals (V_9, V_7, etc.).

All exercises from Chapter XIV should now be treated in a similar manner, disregarding the chords specified in each lesson. In the re-writing of the work of this chapter, the student should attempt a simple harmonization, in which the effort to secure distinct melodic progression for each voice is the principal factor.

Also, from this point on, the student will benefit by writing four-measure phrases in open harmony, using all chords thus far introduced. The purpose of this original work is to stimulate original chord thinking. Let the first efforts be thoroughly simple. Aim for clearness and for as much chord variety as is consistent. When the four-measure phrase form is mastered, the eight measure period should be taken up; the period permits more elasticity in the choice of chords.

Continue original analysis until the following offer no obstacle:

(1) The source of the chord and its impulse in the place it appears.
(2) Chord position.
(3) Preparation and resolution of dissonances.
(4) Identity of cadences.

(5) Presence and purpose of passing tones.
(6) Modulations.
(7) Explanation of all apparently irregular progressions.

If the student has provided himself with a copy of the *Choralbuch*, by August Haupt, he should copy the melody of several chorals in major, and harmonize them without reference to the originals. Then compare chord for chord.

Review the chapter on the ninth chord in Part I of this text. This five-voiced chord must, in these exercises, be employed as a four-voiced chord only. The ninth must be prepared and resolved.

Of the exercises that follow, No. 1 should also be harmonized in F minor; and No. 4, in D minor:

ANALYSIS

A. MARMONTEL

1. Add Roman numerals, two to each measure indicating roots; add Arabic signs indicating position.
2. Distinguish carefully between fundamental chords and inversions.
3. How many ninth chords are employed?
4. Where are secondary sevenths employed?
5. What key enters in measure 13?
6. Does the A♭ in measure 22 create a new key?
7. At what measure is the first phrase repeated?
8. What cadences are employed?

These two quotations from J. G. Albrechtsberger's *Musical Composition* should be analyzed, chord by chord. Note particularly:

(1) The use of the ninth chords.
(2) The preparation and resolution of dissonances.
(3) The use of suspensions.
(4) The use of modulation.

Each chord should be marked with its Roman and Arabic figuration, each new key being indicated by letter at the point of its entrance.

GENERAL REVIEW

1. In what measures of the C major excerpt by Albrechtsberger, do the parts cross?
2. What voices are included in this?
3. Write the dominant ninth chord on B, and resolve it in four parts to a minor triad.
4. What is the key of the second Albrechtsberger selection, above?
5. How do you explain the D major triad, in the final measure?
6. What influence, on the cadence, is produced by the A♭ in measure twenty-two of the Marmontel selection?

CHAPTER XIX

THE LEADING–TONE TRIAD AND SEVENTH CHORD

The vii° and vii°7 are an integral part of the dominant harmony. The vii° is to be regarded as V_7 with root omitted; the vii°7 as V_9 with root omitted. Hence, in the use of these two chords, it is essential to keep the influence of the dominant in mind.

Of the following, transpose No. 1 to B minor; No. 2, to F major.

[Musical exercises with chord indications:]

VII₇   VII   ⁶₄   V₇

4.
⁶₄   VII   VII₇

⁶₄   VII VII₇   IV₇ II₇ I VII   II₇

5.
V₇   VII₇   VII₇   VII₇   VII₇

Harmonize the above exercises twice. The first time disregard the suggested chords and use simple connections. The second time introduce the chords indicated by the Roman numerals. Every given soprano, unlike a bass with chord figuration, admits of many possible harmonizations. It is, consequently, of the greatest importance to use a given subject repeatedly, elaborating the harmonic structure from a simple basis.

The following sequential passage from Albrechtsberger shows the use of the vii$^9_7$.

The vii$^9_7$ in minor:

The vii° in major:

ANALYSIS

1. Where is the Deceptive cadence employed?
2. What keys are suggested and introduced?
3. In what position is the vii° used?
4. What secondary seventh chords are used?
5. Mark all instances of the Suspension.
6. Mark all Passing tones.
7. Are any non-modulatory chromatics introduced?
8. When is it necessary to employ close position?

Felix Mendelssohn-Bartholdy

1. Explain the use of all unisons between any two adjacent parts.
2. Mark all Passing tones.
3. Name the cadence at each Phrase ending.
4. Where do Suspensions occur?
5. In what key is the third Phrase (sixth measure)?
6. What other modulations enter?
7. What is the relation of each modulation to the tonic?
8. Mark each seventh chord, noting preparation and resolution of the seventh.
9. Where is close position used? Why?

CHAPTER XX

THE CHORD ON THE MEDIANT, IN MAJOR

Of the following exercises, Nos. 4 and 5 introduce Sequences (fundamental chord forms). Each exercise should be worked out in a simple form of harmonization. Then again, introducing the chords indicated by the Roman numerals. Review in Part I, the chapter on the Mediant Triad.

113

The Triad of III moving to VI:

The Triad of III moving to IV:

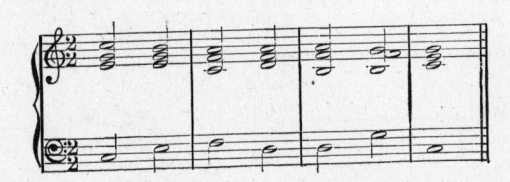

The Triad on III (six chord) in a modulation:

The Triad on III (⁶⁄₄ chord) in modulation:

CHAPTER XXI

MODULATION

Of the exercises to be harmonized, in this chapter, Nos. 1 to 5 present modulations to next-related keys; Nos. 6 to 10 to next-related and to remote keys. Each key entrance is indicated, and essential chords are shown in Roman numerals.

It is only by extending the study of analytical harmony that the pupil can become thoroughly familiar with the influence of chromatics introduced into music. Many compositions contain tones foreign to the key that do not even infer a modulation; again, chromatic tones may be introduced, and a related or a remote key may be clearly suggested but not established; still again, a new key may be made clear without the use of chromatic tones.

The most definite and satisfactory manner of establishing a new key is to introduce its dominant chord (V or V_7). Between the starting point (say, C major) and the desired end point (E minor, for example) there must be a gradual merging of tonalities, becoming definitely established when the V_7 (of E minor) enters.

It is necessary to introduce a chord, or a series of chords, before the new V_7 enters that are common to both keys. For example, in passing from C major to E minor, the triad on A is a valuable bridge chord because it is found both in C major, as VI, and in E minor, as IV. Furthermore, the root of this triad is the seventh of the V_7 of E minor, which again establishes an intimate relationship.

This intimate relationship is the one fact that gives smoothness and naturalness to the entrance of the new key.

By the merging of the starting point key, through chords common to both keys, modulations may be made to sound as natural when remote keys are sought as when the nearly related keys are concerned. Thus, in passing from C major to F♯ (see Appendix), it is only necessary to prepare and connect the key of F♯ through the influence of the tones of C major (E♯–F and B), and the tone-blending is entirely free of any abruptness.

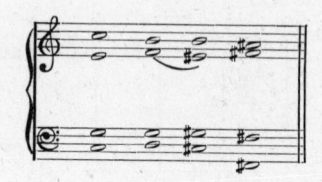

As a general rule, it may be said that a nearly related key may be reached by immediately introducing its V_7 chord, while a remote key may be reached by connecting a triad within the first key with the V_7 of the new key. The two preceding examples illustrate this statement.

Modulations that merely suggest the new key, but do not fully establish it, are called transient.

Modulations may be chromatic or enharmonic. The former embrace those that are brought about by the smooth and satisfactory entrance of the tones of the new key. Enharmonic modulations effect the same purpose but retain a pitch while changing its name. (See the above modulations from C major to F♯ major.)

The following modulations from Albrechtsberger should be analyzed. Note the close connection from chord to chord, and the entire naturalness of the voice progressions.

C major to G major:

C major to F minor:

C major to E♭ major:

C major to A major:

C minor to D♭ major:

EXERCISES TO BE HARMONIZED

Capital letters indicate major keys; small letters, minor keys.

C   G $^6_4$

C V$_7$ $^6_4$

2

B♭
6
4
E♭
VI
g
E♭
B♭
V9

3

f♯
b
A
E
f♯
VII7
VII7

4

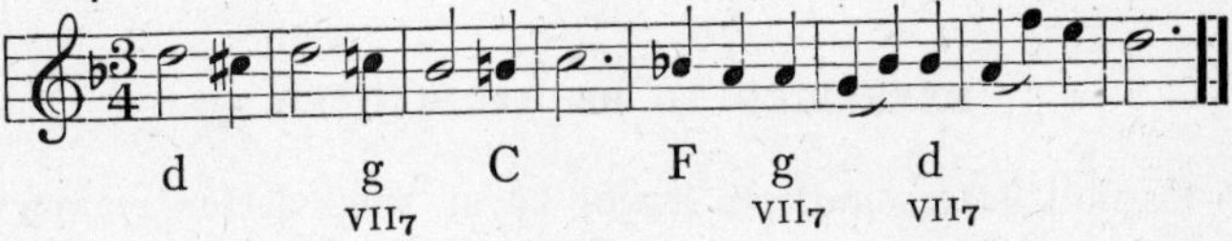
d
g
C
F
g
d
VII7
VII7
VII7

5

D
VII
A
b
VII7
f♯
G
e
D
VII7

6

E
V7
e
a
e
VII7
V7
E

7

A♭
E♭
V7
f
VII7
D♭
A♭
C
e
II7
C
A♭

8

D
g
V
F
a
II7
C
f
a
VII7
D
II7

9

F
b♭
VII7
a♭
VII7
Sequence
B
I
E♭
I
d
V7
II

10

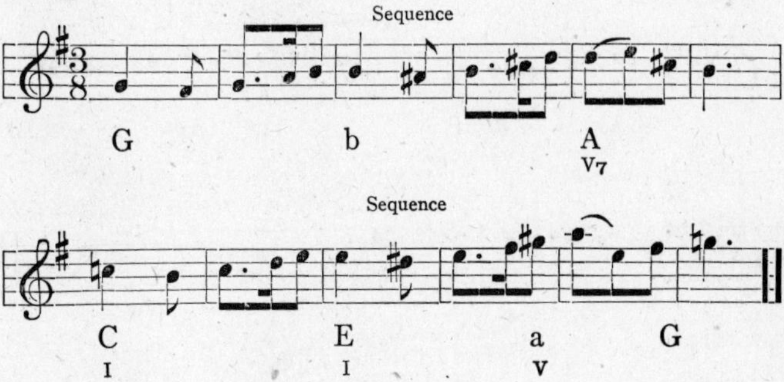
Sequence
G
b
A
V7
Sequence
C
I
E
I
a
V
G

APPENDIX I

TABLE OF SIMPLE CHORD PROGRESSIONS, IN MAJOR

Triad on:	May proceed to:			
I	IV	V	VI	
II	V	VI		
III	I	IV	VI	
IV	I	II	V	
V	I	II	III	VI
VI	II	III	IV	V
VII°	(To be used fundamentally in sequences)			

TABLE OF SIMPLE CHORD PROGRESSIONS, IN MINOR

Triad on:	May proceed to:			
I	IV	V	VI	
II°	V			
III+	I	V	VI	
IV	I	II°	V	VI
V	I	III+	IV	VI
VI	I	II°	III+	IV
VII°	(See VII° under major scale triads)			

The student should review the rules and models in each chapter of "FIRST YEAR HARMONY" (omitting the chapter on Melody Writing), and construct original basses for harmonization in four parts, close position. This should be followed by a review of the same material written in open position.

The chords to be taken up in this original writing of basses (and later of the soprano part) are:

1. Fundamental triads in major.
2. Fundamental triads in minor.
3. The six chord (in major and minor).
4. The four-six chord (in major and minor).
5. The V^7 fundamentally.
6. The inversions of the V^7 ($^6_5$ $^6_4$ $^6_3$ $^6_2$).
7. The various sevenths in the order in which they are presented in Part I of this book.

For the first attempt in writing original basses, use only the four measure phrase form. For final cadence, both the Authentic and Plagal forms should be introduced.

MODULATIONS

(See Chapter XXI):

1. Original modulations, at first as brief in extent as possible, should be made at the keyboard.
2. For the first effort, let the modulation take place from C major, as a starting point, and proceed to every other major key. Thus: C to D♭, C to D, C to E♭, C to E, etc.
3. Such brief modulations may be limited to three or four chords. Thus, from C major to F♯ major. The first chord is C major, the *last* chord will be F♯ major, the penultimate chord will be the V^7 of F♯ major. A connecting chord between C major and the V^7 of F♯ major is required for smoothness. In all cases the connecting chord must contain one or more tones in common with the V^7 chord of the new key. Thus:

a.

C   V$_7$ F♯ V$_7$

4. Many brief modulations require but three chords. In such cases it will be found that the V^7 chord of the new key is intimately related or connected with the first chord. Thus:

b.

C maj.   I   F V$_7$ I
             maj.

5. These brief modulations should be first worked out at the keyboard, and then written in correct four-part, open position, harmony.

6. Once this simple mechanism is mastered, the modulation should be carried out over a greater number of measures, preferably in the four-measure phrase form.

APPENDIX II

EXAMINATION PAPERS

A. The New York State Education Department

HARMONY

Candidates are required to answer six questions from this group.

1. Figure and resolve *each* of the following chords:

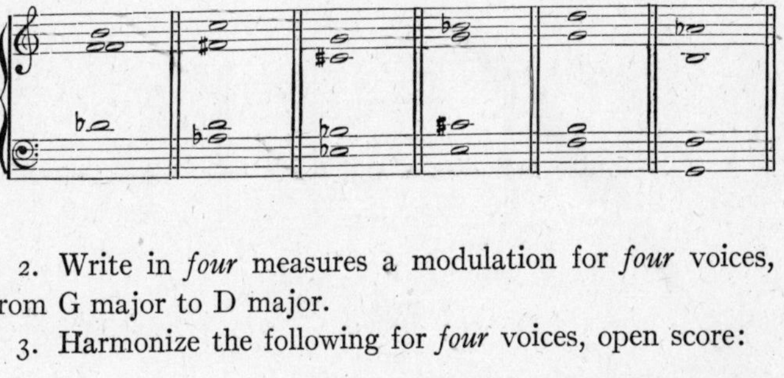

2. Write in *four* measures a modulation for *four* voices, from G major to D major.

3. Harmonize the following for *four* voices, open score:

4. Harmonize the following bass for *four* voices, close position:

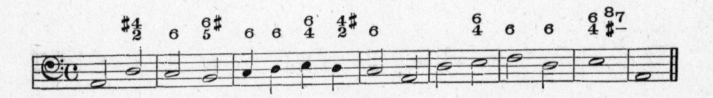

5. Resolve *each* of the following chords in *two* ways, giving in each case the name of the resolution and the key:

6. Add soprano, alto and tenor to the following unfigured bass; any chords or inversions may be used:

7. Harmonize melodies *a* and *b* for *four* voices, in short score:

8. Illustrate with *three* chords, the following suspensions:

4–3	9–8	7–6	9–8	9–8
			4–3	7–6

B. Associate Examination Paper set by the American College of Musicians

1. Write in four voices and resolve a diminished triad and an augmented triad.

2. Classify, figure and resolve the following:

3. Progress by good voice-leading, from the following chord (triad of F major) directly (*i.e.*, without intervening chord) into the dominant seventh chord, which will resolve primarily into the triads of: (*a*) G flat major; (*b*) D minor; (*c*) B flat major; (*d*) C minor. Work this test similar to the following illustration. Any position of the Dominant seventh is available.

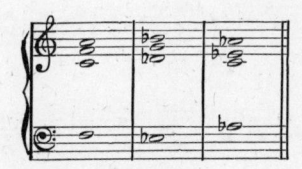

4. Modulate from G major to E flat major by means of triads only. Finish with complete cadence. Modulate back to G major in the same manner. Finish with complete cadence.

5. Illustrate suspensions. Give rules therefor. Figure your examples.

6. Give example of diminished seventh chord. Resolve it.

7. Mention any other kind of chord that is not included in the foregoing example.

8. Harmonize in four voices the following Cantus. Employ sufficient embellishments, passing notes, etc., to secure smooth movement.

C. Fellowship Examination Paper: American College of Musicians

1. Harmonize following bass in four parts. The letters represent the roots of chords to be used. Roots, however, do not always appear in the bass. Capitals represent major chords, small letters minor chords.

2. And the following melody in four parts. Additional parts may be embellished.

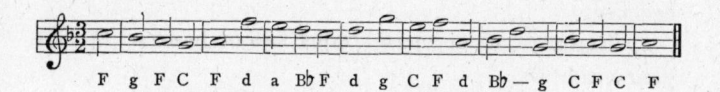

F g F C   F d a B♭ F   d g C F d B♭ — g   C F C   F

3. Harmonize the following bass in four parts. Additional parts may be embellished.

4. And the following melody in four parts. Additional voices may be embellished (imitation, etc.).

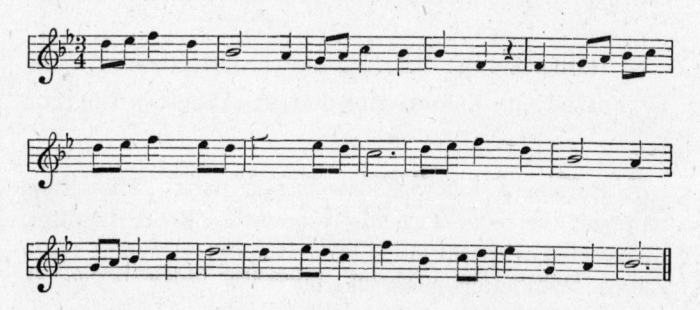

5. Take same melody and write free piano accompaniment.

6. Write and harmonize in four parts an original melody of eight or more measures.

7. Give some general principles which you would carry out in teaching modulation.

8. Resolve each of the following two or more ways. Indicate keys and give explanations.

D. GENERAL HARMONY TEST. NO. 1.

1. Harmonize the following chord-scheme. Key of C minor: $\frac{4}{4}$.

$$V \mid I - II^o \text{ att.} \mid V - VI \text{ att.} \mid IV \text{ att. } VI \text{ att.} \mid I_{II} \; V^7 \; I \, \|.$$

2. Harmonize the following melody, using as few chord as possible and some non-harmonic effects.

3. Complete the following 4-measure cadence-group in two different ways; (*a*) by a modulation into a minor key; (*b*) by a modulation, effected by means of a hinge-chord which shall be chromatic in both keys.

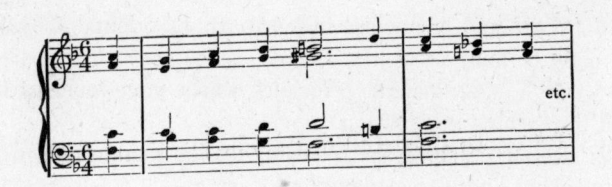

Harmonize this melody in two ways, completing the exercise with a modulation. Notate all chords.

(a) Harmonize the melody in a *minor* key. Consider the last note (a) as part of a hinge-chord that is chromatic in the first key and diatonic in the second.

(b) Harmonize the melody in a *major* key. Consider the last note (a) as the root of a diminished seventh chord, then by changing this chord enharmonically, make a modulation.

Write three exercises using these chords and notate all the material.

(a) Introduce attendant chords to any four of these chords.

(b) Introduce passing notes, and one or more suspensions and appoggiaturas.

(c) Introduce a pedal point and one major-minor effect.

E. GENERAL HARMONY TEST. No. 2.

1. Define: (a) Note, (b) Staff, (c) Sharp and (d) give the rule for II to I$_4^6$; (e) rule for V to VI in minor. Illustrate (d) and (e) with examples.

2. Write and name the twenty-three used intervals from F♯.

3. Write a major, minor, diminished and augmented triad on E♭ and the table of all the keys in which they are found. (In this and all the remaining questions the proper contrast in size of the chord numerals, etc., is imperative.)

4. Harmonize and letter fully.

5. Harmonize with I, IV and V only, and at + show the four different ways of using a $_4^6$ chord correctly.

F. Test in Chord Construction

1. Construct the diminished seventh chord on C♯, and resolve in two ways.

2. Construct an augmented $\frac{6}{3}$ on E♭, and resolve in two ways.

3. Write as a four-voiced chord the V_9 of G major, E minor, B major, and resolve.

4. Illustrate the preparation and resolution of the following chords in E♭ major: I_7 IV_7.

5. Write a melody embodying the chord progression V VI.

6. Write a melody illustrating the resolution of the II_7 chord.

7. Use the V_7 chord in E minor resolving otherwise than to the tonic.

8. Write in four parts, the chord succession I V_9 V_7 I.

9. Illustrate the use of the $^6_4$ as the passing chord.

10. Resolve the V_7 of any major key so that the seventh (which should be placed in the soprano) will proceed as follows:

   (a) Up an augmented prime.
   (b) Up a major second.
   (c) Remain stationary.

11. Resolve the V_7 (as in No. 10) in any minor key.

12. Construct the following on D♭ and resolve at least in two ways: Augmented six-four-three, Augmented six-five-three, Augmented six-three.

First Year Musical Theory

(RUDIMENTS OF MUSIC)

BY

THOMAS TAPPER

Price $1.00

This is a simple, readable text upon all the matter that is generally included in Rudiments of Music.

While the effort of the author has been to make the reading matter of the chapters as thoroughly interesting as the subject permits, the student is assured of gaining all the technical knowledge that is included under the subject matter through the test questions that accompany the various chapters.

The origin of words and symbols as used in music is traced whenever possible. The book abounds in music illustrations which amplify the meaning of the English text. The questions at the end of the various chapters require a considerable amount of written work, and through this requirement, familiarize the student with all the technical features of musical notation.

The book is valuable as a reference source. It contains a well-selected list of musical terms. All the major scales are given in tabular form. The three forms of the minor scales are similarly presented, and the book, in conclusion, presents a number of test papers actually set in schools, colleges, and universities, indicating to what extent musical theory is required in institutions of higher learning as preparatory knowledge.

FIRST YEAR ANALYSIS
(MUSICAL FORM)
BY
THOMAS TAPPER
Price $1.00

A PRACTICAL text on the Forms in music.
 Following the introductory chapters on the elements of Form (Motive, Phrase, Period), the smaller forms are taken up and analysis is required as a basis of further familiarity with the constructive plan underlying the form in question.

As most text-books on Musical Form merely recommend that analysis be done by the student, it is generally the case that the music assigned for analysis is either not at hand, or hard to obtain. To obviate this and to make it certain that there will be no impediment to the actual performance of the required analysis, *all examples are printed in a separate book as a supplement to this volume, entitled "Form and Analysis."*

The advantage of having all the required forms in one collection as against having to find them in many volumes is obvious.

"FORM AND ANALYSIS"
SUPPLEMENTARY MATERIAL TO
FIRST YEAR ANALYSIS
FINGERED AND EDITED BY
THOMAS TAPPER
(*Schmidt's Educational Series, No. 122*)

PRICE 75 CENTS